BERGERE
DE FRANCE

Baby Booties and Socks:

50 Knits for Tiny Toes

Frédérique Alexandre

As a child, Frédérique Alexandre was taught to sew and crochet by her mother, aunts and grandmother during long summer holidays in the countryside. She grew up loving to create dolls, cushions and multi-coloured patchwork blankets and has carried this passion for craft into her adult life.

Frédérique studied Decorative Arts at the Sèvres Technical School then completed a Textile Creation vocational training certificate at the Duperré School in Paris. For the last 28 years she has been working as a freelance designer for various wool manufacturers and publishers within France. She has a fond passion for baby and children's designs and now works almost exclusively in this area.

First published in Great Britain in 2013 by Search Press Limited, Wellwood, North Farm Road, Tunbridge Wells, Kent, TN2 3DR

Original title: *Chassons de bébé* © 2012 by Éditions Marie Claire- Société d'Information et de Création (SIC)
World rights reserved by Éditions Marie Claire

Design and creations provided by Bergère de France and Frédérique Alexandre
Photography by Pierre Nicou
Design and layout by Either Studio

English translation by Burravoe Translation Services

English edition produced by GreenGate Publishing Services, Tonbridge

ISBN: 978-1-84448-995-4

Printed in Malaysia

Suppliers:
This book was sponsored by Bergère de France who supplied all the yarn materials used by the author in these projects. Bergère de France provides an on-line ordering facility and distributes worldwide. However, all of the yarns used in this book can be readily obtained from alternative sources, including specialist stores, on-line suppliers and mail-order companies.

Baby Booties and Socks:

50 Knits for Tiny Toes

Frédérique Alexandre

SEARCH PRESS

Contents

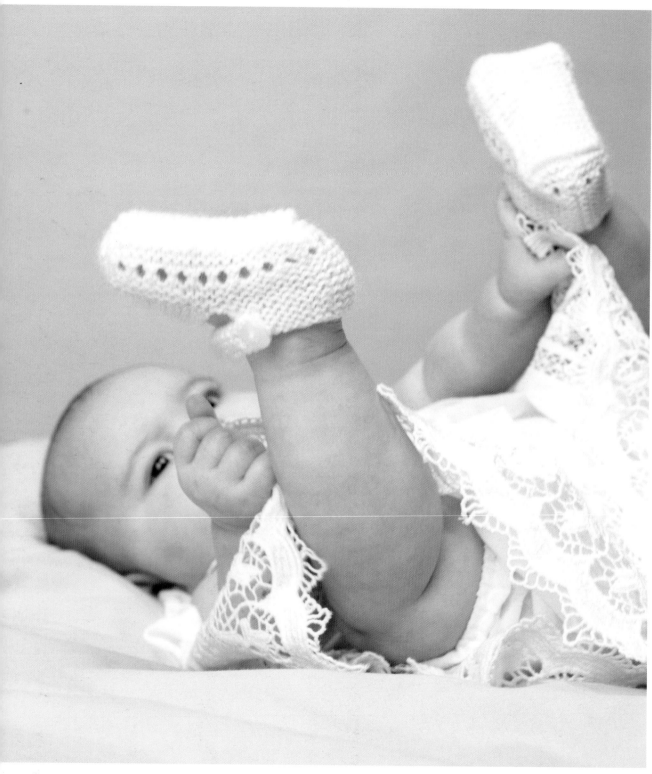

For Special Occasions

1 Garter-stitch Delights

2 Sweet and Simple

Garter–stitch Delights

SIZES

Newborn/1 month • 3 months • 6 months (instructions for the two larger sizes are given in brackets)

MATERIALS

1 ball of Bergère de France Caline (or similar easy-care baby/fingering yarn) in Jerry (mid-grey) • 50cm (½yd) of reversible spotted ribbon • 2.5mm (UK 12; US 2) knitting needles • 2 small round buttons • 3 stitch holders

STITCHES

Double decrease, centred (sl2, k1, p2sso): See page 154.
Garter stitch: Knit every row.

GAUGE

27 sts and 54 rows in garter stitch on 2.5mm (UK 12; US 2) knitting needles = 10 × 10cm (4 × 4in).
Note: Use smaller needles if your sample works out bigger than this; use bigger needles if your sample works out smaller than this.

METHOD

Start at the top.
Cast on 25 (29, 33) sts. Work 4cm (5cm, 6cm)/1½in (2in, 2¼in), i.e. 23 (27, 33) rows, in garter stitch.

INSTEP

Slip 9 (10, 11) sts at each side on to stitch holders. Work 14 (16, 18) rows in garter stitch on the 7 (9, 11) central sts. Leave these sts on a holder.

SIDES

Next row: Knit the 9 (10, 11) sts from the holder on the right, pick up and knit 8 (9, 10) sts along the right edge of the instep, knit the 7 (8, 9) sts from the middle holder, pick up and knit 8 (9, 10) sts along the left edge of the instep and then knit the 9 (10, 11) sts from the holder on the left [41 (47, 53) sts].
Work 10 (12, 14) rows in garter stitch on these 41 (47, 53) sts.

SOLE

Next row: K3 (5, 6), sl2, k1, p2sso, k8 (9, 10), sl2, k1, p2sso, k7 (8, 9), sl2, k1, p2sso, k8 (9, 10), sl2, k1, p2sso, k3 (4, 6).
Continue to work the sole, repeating these decreases once more on the 4th row and twice every 2nd row after that, working 1 st less at the beginning and end of the row and 2 sts less between each double decrease.
On the 2nd following row, cast off the remaining 9 (15, 21) sts.

FINISHING

Sew up the bootie, allowing for a turnover at the top. Now make a second bootie to match.
For the bows, cut the ribbon in half and tie a bow with each piece. Trim the ends of the ribbon as desired. Stitch a bow in place on the front of each bootie with a button on top.

TIP

If you haven't made a pair of baby booties before, these are the ideal first project because they are worked completely in knit stitch and have a simple construction.

Sweet and Simple

SIZES

Newborn/1 month • 3 months • 6 months (instructions for the two larger sizes are given in brackets)

MATERIALS

1 ball of Bergère de France Caline (or similar easy-care baby/fingering yarn) in Nono (steel grey) • 80m (1yd) reversible spotted ribbon • 2.5mm (UK 12; US 2) and 3mm (UK 11; US 3) knitting needles • 3 stitch holders

STITCHES

Double decrease, centred (sl2, k1, p2sso): See page 154.
K1 p1 rib: *K1, p1* repeat from * to * to the end.
Seed stitch (requires an odd number of sts):
 Row 1: *K1, p1*, repeat from * to * to the end, finishing with k1.
 Row 2: *P1, k1*, repeat from * to * to the end, finishing with p1.
 Repeat these two rows.
Stocking stitch: Knit right-side rows, purl wrong-side rows.

GAUGE

27 sts and 36 rows in stocking stitch on 3mm (UK 11; US 3) knitting needles = 10 × 10 cm (4 × 4in).
Note: Use smaller needles if your sample works out bigger than this; use bigger needles if your sample works out smaller.

METHOD

Start at the top.
Using 3mm (UK 11; US 3) knitting needles, cast on 31 (35, 39) sts. Work 16 rows in seed stitch.
Change to 2.5mm (UK 12; US 2) needles and work 6 rows in k1 p1 rib.
Change to 3mm (UK 11; US 3) needles and work 4 (6, 8) rows stocking stitch.

INSTEP

Slip 11 (13, 15) sts at each side on to stitch holders. Work 14 (16, 18) rows in stocking stitch on the 9 central sts. Leave these sts on a holder.

SIDES

Knit the 11 (13, 15) sts from the holder on the right, pick up and knit 10 (11, 12) sts along the right edge of the instep, knit the 9 sts from the middle holder, pick up and knit 10 (11, 12) sts along the left edge of the instep and then knit the 11 (13, 15) sts from the holder on the left [51 (57, 63) sts]. Work 8 rows in stocking stitch on these 51 (57, 63) sts.

SOLE

Continue in seed stitch as follows: Work 4 (5, 5) sts, sl2, k1, p2sso, work 11 (13, 15) sts, sl2, k1, p2sso, work 9 (10, 11) sts, sl2, k1, p2sso, k11 (13, 15) sts, sl2, k1, p2sso, work 4 (4, 5) sts.
Continue to work the sole, repeating these decreases once more on the 4th row and twice every 2nd row after that, working 1 st less at the beginning and end of the row and 2 sts less between each double decrease.
On the 2nd following row, cast off all remaining sts.

FINISHING

Sew up the bootie, allowing for a turn-down cuff at the top.
Make a second bootie to match.
For the bows, cut the ribbon in half and tie a bow with each piece. Trim the ends of the ribbon as desired. Stitch a bow in place on the front of each bootie.

3 Stars and Stripes

4 Baby Blue

Stars and Stripes

SIZES

Extra-small • Newborn • 1 month • 3 months • 6 months (instructions for the four larger sizes are given in brackets)

MATERIALS

1 ball each of Bergère de France Caline (or similar easy-care baby/fingering yarn) in Jerry (mid-grey) and Baby (blue) • 2.5mm (UK 12; US 2) and 3mm (UK 11; US 3) knitting needles • 2 star-shaped mother-of-pearl buttons

STITCHES

Double decrease, centred (sl2, k1, p2sso): See page 154.
Garter stitch: Knit every row.
Increase 1 (inc 1): See page 156.
K2 p2 rib: *K2, p2* repeat from * to * to the end.
Stocking stitch: Knit right-side rows, purl wrong-side rows.

GAUGE

27 sts and 36 rows in stocking stitch on 3mm (UK 11; US 3) knitting needles = 10 × 10cm (4 × 4in).
Note: Use smaller needles if your sample works out bigger than this; use bigger needles if your sample works out smaller.

METHOD

Start with the sole.
Using 3mm (UK 11; US 3) needles and mid-grey yarn, cast on 21 (25, 29, 33, 37) sts. Work 2 rows in garter stitch.
Row 3: K1, inc 1, k9 (11, 13, 15, 17), inc 1, k1, inc 1, k9 (11, 13, 15, 17), inc 1, k1 [25 (29, 33, 37, 41) sts].
Row 4: Knit.
Row 5: K2, inc 1, k9 (11, 13, 15, 17), inc 1, k3, inc 1, k9 (11, 13, 15, 17, 19), inc 1 k2 [29 (33, 37, 41, 45) sts].
Row 6: Knit.
Repeat these increases twice more, knitting 1 more stitch before the first increase and after the last increase and 2 more stitches between the 2nd and 3rd increases [37 (41, 45, 49, 53 sts)].
Work 3 (3, 3, 5, 5) rows without increasing.

UPPER

Next row: Using blue, k17 (19, 21, 23, 25), sl2, k1, p2sso, k17 (19, 21, 23, 25).
Next row: Using blue, purl [35 (39, 43, 47, 51) sts].
Next row: Using mid-grey, k16 (18, 20, 22, 24), sl2, k1, p2sso, k16 (18, 20, 22, 24).
Next row: Using mid-grey, purl [33 (37, 41, 45, 49) sts].
Continue in stocking stitch, repeating these 4 rows and working 1 double decrease on the 3 central stitches 6 more times on every other row.
Work 2 (2, 2, 4, 6) rows on the remaining 21 (25, 29, 33, 37) sts, still in the striped pattern.

TOP BAND

Change to 2.5mm (UK 12; US 2) needles and work k2 p2 rib in blue for 8 rows, increasing 1 st on the first row. Cast off the remaining 22 (26, 30, 34, 38) sts.

FINISHING

Sew up the sole and the back of the bootie and then make a second bootie to match.
Sew a star-shaped butting to the front of each bootie, using the photograph as a guide to positioning.

Baby Blue

SIZES

Newborn • 1 month • 3 months • 6 months (instructions for the three larger sizes are given in brackets)

MATERIALS

1 ball of Bergère de France Ciboulette (or similar easy-care baby/fingering yarn) in Aqua (light turquoise) • 2.5mm (UK 12; US 2) knitting needles • Stitch holder • 4 small matching buttons

STITCHES

Double decrease, centred (sl2, k1, p2sso): See page 154.
Garter stitch: Knit every row.
Increase (inc 1): See page 156.
Seed stitch (requires an odd number of sts):
   Row 1: *K1, p1*, repeat from * to * to the end, finishing with k1.
   Row 2: *P1, k1*, repeat from * to * to the end, finishing with p1.
   Repeat these two rows.

GAUGE

31 sts and 42 rows in seed stitch on 2.5mm (UK 12; US 2) knitting needles = 10 × 10cm (4 × 4in).
Note: Use smaller needles if your sample works out bigger than this; use bigger needles if your sample works out smaller.

METHOD

Start with the sole.
Using 2.5mm (UK 12; US 2) knitting needles, cast on 27 (31, 35, 39) sts. Work two rows in seed stitch, starting the 1st row with k1.
Row 3: k1, inc 1, work 12 (14, 16, 18) sts in seed stitch, inc 1, p1, inc 1, work 12 (14, 16, 18) sts in seed stitch, inc 1, work 1 st [31 (35, 39, 43) sts].
Continue in seed stitch, repeating these increases 3 (3, 4, 5) more times, every 2 rows, working two more stitches between the increases each time. For example, row 5 would be: k1, inc 1, work 14 (16, 18, 20) sts in seed stitch, inc 1, p1, inc 1, work 14 (16, 18, 20) sts in seed stitch, inc 1, work 1 st. When you have finished the increases you will have 43 (47, 55, 63) sts. Work 5 (5, 7, 9) rows on these sts.

INSTEP

Still working in seed stitch, work 20 (22, 26, 30) sts, sl2, k1, p2sso, work 20 (22, 26, 30) sts.
Repeat this decrease every 2 rows until 23 (27, 33, 39) sts remain. Work 1 row.

CUFF

Continuing on in seed stitch, work 11 (13, 16, 19) sts, knit twice into next st, work 11 (13, 16, 19) sts. Leave the 12 (14, 17, 20) sts at the left on a stitch holder and work 8 (10, 12, 14) rows in seed stitch on the remaining sts. Cast off. Slip the 12 (14, 17, 20) sts on the stitch holder on to your needles and work 8 (10, 12, 14) rows of seed stitch. Cast off.

FINISHING

Sew up the seams and then make a second bootie to match.
Stitch two buttons to the front of each bootie, using the photographs as a guide to positioning.

5 All Square

6 Elegant Simplicity

5 All Square

SIZES

Newborn/1 month • 3 months • 6 months (instructions for the two larger sizes are given in brackets)

MATERIALS

1 ball each of Bergère de France Ciboulette (or similar easy-care baby/fingering yarn) in Diamant (white) and Aquilon (light blue) • 2.5mm (UK 12; US 2) knitting needles • 2 small white heart-shaped buttons • 3 stitch holders

STITCHES

Garter stitch: Knit every row.
Grafting: See page 155.
K2 p2 rib: *K2, p2*, repeat from * to * to the end.

GAUGE

29 sts and 54 rows in garter stitch on 2.5mm (UK 12; US 2) knitting needles = 10 × 10cm (4 × 4in).
Note: Use smaller needles if your sample works out bigger than this; use bigger needles if your sample works out smaller.

METHOD

Begin at the top.
Using white yarn, cast on 42 (46, 50) sts. Work 6cm (2½in), i.e. 29 rows, in k2 p2 rib.

INSTEP

Slip 16 (18, 20) sts at each side on to stitch holders.
Change to blue and work 14 (16, 18) rows in garter stitch on the 10 central sts. Leave these sts on a stitch holder.

SIDES

Knit the 16 (18, 20) sts from the holder on the right, pick up and knit 9 (10, 11) sts along the right edge of the instep, knit the 10 sts from the middle holder, pick up and knit 9 (10, 11) sts along the left edge of the instep and then knit the 16 (18, 20) sts from the holder on the left [60 (66, 72) sts].
Work 10 (10, 12) rows in garter stitch on these 60 (66, 72) sts.

SOLE

Slip 25 (28, 31) sts at each side on to stitch holders. Continue in garter stitch on the 10 central sts, on each row, knitting together the last stitch on the needle with the first stitch from the adjacent holder.
When five stitches remain on the holders on each side, join the bootie together by grafting these sts to the 10 sts of the instep (see page 155).

FINISHING

Sew up the back seam of the bootie, allowing for a 3cm (1¼in) turn-down cuff at the top.
Knit a second bootie in the same way.
Sew a button on the outside of each bootie, holding the two layers of the cuff in place.

Elegant Simplicity

SIZES

Newborn/1 month • 3 months • 6 months (instructions for the two larger sizes are given in brackets)

MATERIALS

1 ball of Bergère de France Caline (or similar easy-care baby/fingering yarn) in Chausson (pale blue) • 80cm (1yd) matching Vichy ribbon • 3mm (UK 11; US 3) knitting needles

STITCHES

Double decrease, left slanted (sl1, k2tog, psso): See page 155.
Garter stitch: Knit every row.
Increase 1 (inc 1): See page 156.
Single decrease, right slanted (k2tog): See page 154.
Stocking stitch: Knit right-side rows, purl wrong-side rows.

GAUGE

27 sts and 36 rows in stocking stitch on 3mm (UK 11; US 3) knitting needles = 10 × 10cm (4 × 4in).
Note: Use smaller needles if your sample works out bigger than this; use bigger needles if your sample works out smaller.

METHOD

Begin at the sole.
Using 3mm (UK 11; US 3) needles, cast on 37 (41, 45) sts. Work in stocking stitch for two rows.
Row 3: K1, inc 1, k17 (19, 21), inc 1, k1, inc 1, k17 (19, 21), inc 1, k1.
Row 4: Purl [41 (45, 49) sts].
Row 5: K2, inc 1, k17 (19, 21), inc 1, k3, inc 1, k17 (19, 21), inc 1, k2.
Row 6: Purl [45 (49, 53) sts].
Row 7: K3, inc 1, k17 (19, 21), inc 1, k5, inc 1, k17 (19, 21), inc 1, k3.
Row 8: Purl [49 (53, 57) sts].
Work 4 rows in garter stitch on these 49 (53, 57) sts, followed by 6 (8, 10) rows in stocking stitch.

UPPER

Next row: K21 (23, 25), 1 single decrease, 1 double decrease, k2tog, k 21 (23, 25).
Next row: Purl [45 (49, 53) sts].
Next row: K19 (21, 23), 1 single decrease, 1 double decrease, k2tog, k19 (21, 23).
Next row: Purl [41 (45, 49) sts].
Decrease in the same way every 2 rows 3 more times, knitting two sts less at the beginning and end of each decrease row [29 (33, 37) sts].

CUFF

After these decrease rows, make a row of eyelets as follows:
K2, *yarn over needle (yon), k2tog, k2*, repeat from * to * 6 (7, 8) times and finish with yon, k2tog, k1.
Next row: Purl.
Work a further 8 (10, 12) rows stocking stitch for the cuff.

FINISHING

Sew up the seams on the sole and back and then make a second bootie to match.
Cut the ribbon in half. Thread one piece through the eyelets on each bootie, starting and finishing at the centre front. Tie the ends in a bow and trim them as desired.

7 Little Ballerina

8 Comfy Pumps

Little Ballerina

SIZES

Newborn/1 month • 3 months • 6 months (instructions for the two larger sizes are given in brackets)

MATERIALS

I ball of Bergère de France Idéal (or similar easy-care double knitting yarn) in Danseuse (pink) • 3mm (UK 11; US 3) knitting needles • 15cm (6in) Liberty pink floral bias binding • 4 pink flower-shaped buttons • 10 cm (4in) elastic cord

STITCHES

Garter stitch: Knit every row.
Increase (inc 1): See page 156.
Single decrease, left slanted (sl1, k1, psso): See page 154.
Single decrease, right slanted (k2tog): See page 154.

GAUGE

22 sts and 44 rows in garter stitch on 3mm (UK 11; US 3) knitting needles = 10 × 10cm (4 × 4in).
Note: Use smaller needles if your sample works out bigger than this; use bigger needles if your sample works out smaller.

METHOD

Begin at the sole.
Using 3mm (UK 11; US 3) knitting needles, cast on 35 (37, 43) sts. Work 2 rows in garter stitch.
Row 3: K1, inc 1, k16 (18, 20), inc 1, k1, inc 1, k16 (18, 20), inc 1, k1.
Row 4: Knit [39 (43, 47) sts].
Row 5: K2, inc 1, k16 (18, 20), inc 1, k3, inc 1, k16 (18, 20), inc 1, k2.
Row 6: Knit [43 (47, 51) sts].
Row 7: K3, inc 1, k16 (18, 20), inc 1, k5, inc 1, k16 (18, 20), inc 1, k3.
Row 8: Knit [47 (51, 55) sts].
Work another 12 (14, 16) rows in garter stitch without shaping.

UPPER

Next row: K11 (13, 15) *sl1, k1, psso* 6 times, k1 (centre stitch), k2tog 6 times, k11 (13, 15) [35 (39, 43) sts].
Work 2 rows in garter stitch.
Cast off all sts on the following row.
Sew up the sole and heel.

SLIPPER BAND

Cut a 6cm (2½in) length of bias binding. Sew one end to one side of the bootie with a button. Cut a short length of elastic cord and sew one end to the bias binding and the other end to the second side of the bootie with another button.

Make a second bootie, reversing the direction of the button band.

Comfy Pumps

SIZES

Newborn/1 month • 3 months • 6 months (instructions for the two larger sizes are given in brackets)

MATERIALS

1 ball each of Bergère de France Ciboulette (or similar easy-care baby/fingering yarn) in Barbie (pale pink) and Diamont (white) • 2.5mm (UK 12; US 2) knitting needles • Stitch holder

STITCHES

Garter stitch: Knit every row.
Increase (inc 1): See page 156.
Single decrease, left slanted (sl1, k1, psso): See page 154.
Single decrease, right slanted (k2tog): See page 154.

GAUGE

27 sts and 54 rows in garter stitch on 2.5mm (UK 12; US 2) knitting needles = 10 × 10cm (4 × 4in).

Note: Use smaller needles if your sample works out bigger than this; use bigger needles if your sample works out smaller.

METHOD

Start with the sole.
Using pink yarn, cast on 10 (12, 14) sts.
Work 6cm (6.5cm, 7cm)/2⅜in (2½in, 2¾in), i.e. 32 (34, 36) rows, in garter stitch. Leave the stitches on a stitch holder.

FOOT

Using pink yarn, cast on 5 (6, 6) sts, pick up and knit 14 (15, 16) sts along the right edge of the sole, knit the 10 (12, 14) sts from the holder, pick up and knit 14 (15, 16) sts along the left edge of the sole, and then cast on 5 (6, 6) sts [48 (54, 58) sts].
Work 12 (14, 16) rows garter stitch on these stitches.

INSTEP

Knit 28 (32, 35) sts, sl1, k1, psso, turn.
Next row: K9 (11, 13) sts, k2tog, turn.
Next row: K9 (11, 13) sts, sl1, k1, psso, turn.
Repeat the last 2 rows until there are 14 (15, 16) sts remaining on either side of the 8 (10, 12) central stitches.
After the last decrease, turn and knit the 9 (11, 13) sts of the instep and the 14 (15, 16) sts on the left [36 (40, 44) sts].
Next row: Using white, knit 1 row across all stitches.
Next row: Cast off, and as you do so, pull in the edge by working k1 (2, 2) sts, k2tog, k5 (5, 6) sts, k2tog, k5 (5, 6) sts, k2tog, and so on, finishing with k5 (8, 8).

FINISHING

Sew up the back seam and then join the sole to the 5 (6, 6) sts cast on at each side of the foot.
Make a second slipper to match.

KNITTED BOWS

Using white yarn, cast on 20 sts and work 9 rows in garter stitch. Cast off all stitches. Make a second strip in the same way.
Take one strip and join the two short sides. Arrange the seam at the centre back. Squeeze the middle and sew the bow to the top of one slipper. Attach a second bow to the other slipper in the same way.

9 Lovely in Lilac

Lovely in Lilac

SIZES

Newborn/1 month • 3 months • 6 months (instructions for the two larger sizes are given in brackets)

MATERIALS

1 ball of Bergère de France Ciboulette (or similar easy-care baby/fingering yarn) in Aster (lilac) • 2.5mm (UK 12; US 2) knitting needles • Cable needle • Stitch holder • 2 small lilac buttons • 60cm (¾yd) matching organdie ribbon, 15mm (⅝in) wide

STITCHES

Cable (over 4 sts):

Rows 1 and 3 (right side): Knit.

All even-numbered rows: Purl.

Row 5 (cable row): Slip 2 sts on to cable needle and leave at front of work; knit the next 2 sts, then knit the 2 sts from the cable needle.

Row 7: Knit.

Garter stitch: Knit every row.

Double decrease, centred (sl2, k1, p2sso): See page 154.

Grafting: See page 155.

Stocking stitch: Knit right-side rows, purl wrong-side rows.

GAUGE

31 sts and 42 rows in garter stitch on 2.5mm (UK 12; US 2) needles = 10 × 10cm (4 × 4in).

Note: Use smaller needles if your sample works out bigger than this; use bigger needles if your sample works out smaller.

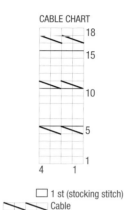

CABLE CHART

1 st (stocking stitch)

Cable

METHOD

Start with the instep. Cast on 12 sts.

Odd rows: K2, p2 then work the cable pattern over 4 sts and end with p2, k2.

Even rows: P2, k2, p4, k2, p2.

When work measures 3.5cm (4cm, 4.5cm)/1⅜in (1½in, 1¾in), i.e. 14 (16, 18 rows), transfer the stitches to a stitch holder.

FOOT

Cast on 11 (12, 13) sts, pick up and knit 9 (10, 11) sts along the right edge of the instep, knit the 12 sts from the holder, pick up and knit 9 (10, 11) sts along the left edge of the instep and then cast on 11 (12, 13) sts [52 (56, 60) sts]. Work 10 (12, 14) rows in stocking stitch on these stitches.

SOLE

Continue in garter stitch as follows: k4, sl2, k1, p2sso, k13 (15, 17), sl2, k1, p2sso, k6, sl2, k1, p2sso, k13 (15, 17), sl2, k1, p2sso, k4. Repeat these decreases twice more, every 4 rows, and then again once more after the next two rows, working one stitch less at the beginning and end of the row and 2 stitches less between each double decrease, so the decreases are positioned above one another. Fasten off the remaining stitches by grafting.

Sew up the back seam.

FRONT LOOP

Pick up 4 sts at the top centre front. Work 16 rows in stocking stitch and cast off. Fold the loop back on itself and stitch down.

RIGHT STRAP

Pick up 20 (22, 24) sts around the back of the bootie and then cast on 16 sts. Work 4 rows in garter stitch.

Row 5: Make a buttonhole over 1 stitch, 2 sts from the edge by working k2tog, yon, knit to the end of the row.

Work 3 more rows in garter stitch. Cast off.

Thread the strap through the front loop. Sew on the button to correspond with the buttonhole.

FINISHING

Make a second bootie, reversing the strap and button.

Cut the ribbon in half and thread one piece through each bootie, behind the first twist of the cable. Tie in a bow and trim the ends as desired.

Eyelet Delights

SIZES

Newborn/1 month • 3 months • 6 months (instructions for the two larger sizes are given in brackets)

MATERIALS

1 ball of Bergère de France Ciboulette (or similar easy-care baby/fingering yarn) in Diamant (white) • 2.5mm (UK 12; US 2) knitting needles • 3 stitch holders • 2 white heart-shaped pearl buttons

STITCHES

Garter stitch: Knit every row.
Grafting: see page 155.
Knit two together (k2tog): See page 154.

GAUGE

31 sts and 42 rows in garter stitch on 2.5mm (UK 12; US 2) knitting needles = 10 × 10cm (4 × 4in).
Note: Use smaller needles if your sample works out bigger than this; use bigger needles if your sample works out smaller.

METHOD

Start with the strap.

Cast on 27 (29, 31) sts and work 3 rows in garter stitch.

Row 4: Make a buttonhole 2 sts in from the beginning of the row by working k2tog, yon, knit to end of row.

Knit 3 rows.

Row 8: Cast off 15 sts and continue on the remaining 12 (14, 16) sts.

Work 3 rows in garter stitch and then slip the stitches on to a stitch holder.

For the back, cast on 12 (14, 16) sts, work 11 rows garter stitch and then slip the stitches on to a stitch holder.

UPPER

Cast on 12 sts, work 20 (22, 24) rows in garter stitch and slip the stitches on to a stitch holder.

Knit the 12 (14, 16) sts from the strap on the stitch holder, pick up and knit 8 (10, 12) sts along the right edge of the instep, knit the 12 sts of the instep from the second stitch holder, pick up and knit 8 (10, 12) sts along the left edge of the instep and then knit the 12 (14, 16) stitches from the back piece (without the buttonhole) from the holder [52 (60, 68) sts].

Work 4 rows in garter stitch on these stitches.

Row 5 (eyelet row): K1, *yon, k2tog*, repeat from * to *, ending with k1.

Work 7 more rows in garter stitch. Slip 20 (24, 28) sts at each end on to holders.

SOLE

Continue working in garter stitch on the 12 central stitches, knitting together the last stitch of each row with the first stitch from the adjacent holder.

When 6 stitches remain on each side, join by grafting to the 12 central stitches (see page 155).

FINISHING

Sew up the seam. Attach the button to correspond with the buttonhole.

Make a second bootie, reversing the strap and button.

 Just for Fun

11 Sporty Fun

12 Pompom Power

Sporty Fun

SIZES

1 month • 3 months • 6 months (instructions for the two larger sizes are given in brackets)

MATERIALS

1 ball each of Bergère de France Idéal (or similar easy-care double knitting yarn) in Pavot (red) and Meije (cream) • 3mm (UK 11; US 3) knitting needles • 3mm (UK 11; US D/3) crochet hook

STITCHES

Double decrease, centred (sl2, k1, p2sso): See page 154.
Garter stitch: Knit every row.
Increase 1 (inc 1): See page 156.
Reverse stocking stitch: Purl right-side rows, knit wrong-side rows.
Stocking stitch: Knit right-side rows, purl wrong-side rows.

GAUGE

24 sts and 31 rows in stocking stitch on 3mm (UK 11; US 3) knitting needles = 10 × 10cm (4 × 4in).
Note: Use smaller needles if your sample works out bigger than this; use bigger needles if your sample works out smaller.

METHOD

Start with the sole.
Using red yarn and 3mm (UK 11; US 3) knitting needles, cast on 25 (29, 33) sts. Work 2 rows in garter stitch.
Row 3: K1, inc 1, k11 (13, 15), inc 1, k1, inc 1, k11 (13, 15), inc 1, k1 [29 (33, 37) sts].
Repeat these increases every other row 3 (3, 4) times, working 2 more stitches between the 2nd and 3rd increases each time [41 (45, 53) sts].
Work 5 more rows on these stitches.

UPPER

K19 (21, 25), sl2, k1, p2sso, k19 (21, 15).
Repeat this double decrease every second row 6 (6, 8) times .

CUFF

Work 1 row of purl on the right side of the work, increasing 1 st in the middle of row [28 (32, 36) sts].
Change to reverse stocking stitch for the cuffs. Work 4cm (1½in), i.e. 12 rows, without shaping. Work 4 rows in pattern from the chart, starting at stitch 5 (5, 1) of the chart. Work 2 more rows in stocking stitch using red yarn and cast off all stitches.

FINISHING

Sew up the bootie, allowing for a turn-down cuff of 2.5cm (1in).
Make a second bootie to match.

CORD TIES

Using a 3mm (UK 11; US 3) crochet hook and cream yarn, make a chain 34cm (13½in) long. Slip stitch into each stitch of the chain and fasten off. Repeat to make a second cord. Thread a cord between the stitches of the ankle on each bootie and tie in a bow.

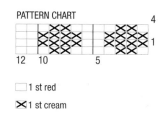

PATTERN CHART

☐ 1 st red
☒ 1 st cream

Pompom Power

SIZES

1 month • 3 months • 6 months (instructions for the two larger sizes are given in brackets)

MATERIALS

1 ball each of Bergère de France Perfection (or similar easy-care baby/fingering yarn) in Gnou (black), Grue (mid-grey) and Chevre (cream) • 2.5mm (UK 12; US 2) and 3mm (UK 11; US 3) knitting needles • 3 stitch holders • 2.5cm (1in) diameter pompom maker

STITCHES

Garter stitch: Knit every row.
Grafting: See page 155.
K1 p1 rib: *K1, p1*, repeat from * to * to the end.
Stocking stitch: Knit right-side rows, purl wrong-side rows.

GAUGE

27 sts and 34 rows in stocking stitch on 3mm (UK 11; US 3) knitting needles = 10 × 10cm (4 × 4in).

Note: Use smaller needles if your sample works out bigger than this; use bigger needles if your sample works out smaller.

METHOD

Start at the top.
Using 2.5mm (UK 12; US 2) needles and mid-grey yarn, cast on 37 (41, 45) sts. Work 6cm (6.5cm, 7cm)/2⅜in (2½in, 2¾in), i.e. 26 (28, 30) rows, in k1 p1 rib. Change to 3mm (UK 11; US 3) needles and work 2 (4, 6) rows in stocking stitch, decreasing 5 sts evenly on the first row [32 (36, 40) sts].

INSTEP

Slip 11 (13, 15) sts each side on to a holder. Change to black yarn and work 8 (10, 12) rows of stocking stitch on the 10 central stitches; slip these stitches on to a holder.

SIDES

Using black yarn, knit the 11 (13, 15) sts from the right-hand holder, pick up and knit 7 (8, 9) sts along the right side of the instep, knit the 10 central stitches from the holder, pick up and knit 7 (8, 9) sts along the left side of the instep and then knit the 11 (13, 15) sts from the left-hand holder [46 (52, 58) sts]. Work 8 (10, 12) rows in stocking stitch on these stitches.

SOLE

Slip 18 (21, 24) sts at each side on to holders. Working in garter stitch and black yarn, knit over the 10 central stitches, knitting together the last stitch of each row with the first stitch from the adjacent holder.
When 5 stitches remain on the holder on each side, join them by grafting to the 10 stitches of the sole (see page 155).

FINISHING

Sew up the bootie, allowing for a 3cm (1¼in) turn-down cuff at the top.
Make a second bootie to match.

POMPOM TRIMS

Make two 2.5cm (1in) diameter pompoms in black and two in mid-grey. Sew one of each colour to the back of each bootie (see the photographs).

14 Tie-ons

Little Imp

SIZES

1 month • 3 months • 6 months (instructions for the two larger sizes are given in brackets)

MATERIALS

1 ball each of Bergère de France Barisienne (or similar easy-care double-knitting yarn) in Caraïbes (deep-sea blue) and Papeete (turquoise) • 6 small ready-made turquoise pompoms • 3mm (UK 11; US 3) and 3.5mm (UK 9; US 4) knitting needles

STITCHES

Double decrease, left slanted (sl2, k1, p2sso): See page 155.
Garter stitch: Knit every row.
Increase 1 (inc 1): See page 156.
Reverse stocking stitch: Purl right-side rows, knit wrong-side rows.
Single decrease, left slanted (sl1, k1, psso): See page 154.
Single decrease, right slanted (k2tog): See page 154.
Stocking stitch: Knit right-side rows, purl wrong-side rows.

GAUGE

22 sts and 30 rows in stocking stitch on 3.5mm (UK 9; US 4) knitting needles = 10 × 10cm (4 × 4in).
Note: Use smaller needles if your sample works out bigger than this; use bigger needles if your sample works out smaller.

METHOD

Start with the sole.
Using blue yarn and 3.5mm (UK 9, US 4) needles, cast on 33 (37, 41) sts.
Row 1: Purl (you will be working in reverse stocking stitch).
Row 2: K1, inc 1, k15 (17, 19), inc 1, k1, inc 1, k15 (17, 19), inc 1, k1.
Row 3: Purl [37 (41, 45) sts].
Row 4: K2, inc 1, k15 (17, 19), inc 1, k3, inc 1, k15 (17, 19), inc 1, k2.
Row 5: Purl [41 (45, 49) sts].
Change to 3mm (UK 11; US 3) needles and turquoise yarn and work 4 rows in garter stitch.

UPPER

Change back to blue yarn and 3.5mm (UK 9; US 4) knitting needles and work 4 (6, 8) rows in stocking stitch.
Next row: Start decreasing as follows: k17 (19, 21), sl1, k1, psso, sl1, k2tog, psso, k2tog, k17 (19, 21).
Next row: Purl [37 (41, 45) sts].
Next row: K15 (17, 19), sl1, k1, psso, sl1, k2tog, psso, k2tog, k15 (17, 19).
Next row: Purl [33 (37, 41) sts].
Repeat these decreases every other row twice, knitting 2 stitches less at the beginning and end of each decrease row [25 (29, 33) sts].
Work 6 (8, 10) rows in stocking stitch on these stitches.

GARTER-STITCH CUFF

Using 3mm (UK 11; US 3) knitting needles and turquoise yarn, cast on 5 (6, 7) sts.
Work in garter stitch, working k1, inc 1 at the right-hand end of every 2nd row until you have 10 (11, 12) sts.
Now work k1, sl1, k1, psso at the right-hand end of every 2nd row until 5 (6, 7) sts. remain.
Repeat until you have worked a total of 3 points.

FINISHING

Sew the cuff to the top of the ankle, remembering that the border will be folded over. Join the seams of the sole and back.
Sew a pompom on each point.
Make a second bootie to match.

14 Tie-ons

SIZES

Newborn/1 month • 3 months • 6 months (instructions for the two larger sizes are given in brackets)

MATERIALS

1 ball of Bergère de France Caline (or similar easy-care baby/fingering yarn) in Hochet (pale turquoise) • 2.5mm (UK 12; US 2) and 3mm (UK 11; US 3) knitting needles • 2 stitch holders

STITCHES

Garter stitch: Knit every row.
Increase 1 (inc 1): See page 156.
Single decrease, left slanted (sl1, k1, psso): See page 154.
Single decrease, right slanted (k2tog): See page 154.
Stocking stitch: Knit right-side rows, purl wrong-side rows.

GAUGE

27 sts and 36 rows in stocking stitch on 3mm (UK 11; US 3) knitting needles = 10 × 10cm (4 × 4in).

Note: Use smaller needles if your sample works out bigger than this; use bigger needles if your sample works out smaller.

METHOD

Start with the sole.

Using 2.5mm (UK 12; US 2) needles, cast on 32 (36, 40) sts. Work in garter stitch as follows:

Row 1: Knit.

Row 2 (wrong side): K1, inc 1, k14 (16, 18), inc 1, k2, inc 1, k14 (16, 18), inc 1, k1 [36 (40, 44) sts].

Row 3: Knit.

Row 4: K2, inc 1, k14 (16, 18), inc 1, k4, inc 1, k14 (16, 18), inc 1, k2 [40 (44, 48) sts].

Repeat these increases 4 more times, on alternate rows as established, working 1 more knit stitch at the beginning and end of the row and 2 more between the 2nd and 3rd increases each time [56 (60, 64) sts].

Work 2 (4, 6) rows in garter stitch.

Change to 3mm (UK 11; US 3) knitting needles and work 2.5cm (1in) in stocking stitch (10 rows).

Next row: K17 (19, 21), *sl1, k1, psso* five times, k2, *k2tog* five times, k17 (19, 21) [46 (50, 54) sts].

Work 3 rows in stocking stitch.

Next row: K17 (19, 21), *sl1, k1, psso* three times, k2, *k2tog* three times, k17 (19, 21) [40 (44, 48) sts].

Work 3 rows in stocking stitch.

Next row: K18 (20, 22), sl1, k1, psso, k2tog, k18 (20, 22) [38 (42, 46) sts].

Work 1 row.

Change to 2.5mm (UK 12; US 2) knitting needles and work 2 rows in garter stitch.

Next row: Knit, slipping 13 (14, 15) sts at each side on to holders.

Work 4 rows on the remaining 10 (12, 14) stitches and cast off.

Knit the 13 (14, 15) sts from the right-hand holder, pick up and knit 4 sts along the 6 rows of garter stitch and then cast on 25 sts (for 1 tie).

Work 5 rows garter stitch on these 42 (43, 44) sts and cast off.

On 2.5mm (UK 12; US 2) needles, cast on 25 sts (for the second tie), pick up and knit 4 sts along the 6 rows of garter stitch and knit the 13 (14, 15) sts from the left-hand holder.

Work 5 rows garter stitch on these 42 (43, 44) sts and cast off.

FINISHING

Sew up the sole and the back of the bootie. Tie the ties in a bow.

Make a second bootie to match.

15 Opposites Attract

16 Black and White

Opposites Attract

SIZES

1 month • 3 months • 6 months (instructions for the two larger sizes are given in brackets)

MATERIALS

1 ball each of Bergère de France Idéal (or similar easy-care double knitting yarn) in Truffle (black) and Everest (white) • 3mm (UK 11; US 3) knitting needles • Tapestry needle

STITCHES

Double decrease, centred (sl2, k1, p2sso): See page 154.
Garter stitch: Knit every row.
Increase 1 (inc 1): See page 156.
Reverse stocking stitch: Purl right-side rows, knit wrong-side rows.
Stocking stitch: Knit right-side rows, purl wrong-side rows.

GAUGE

24 sts and 31 rows in stocking stitch on 3mm (UK 11; US 3) knitting needles = 10 × 10cm (4 × 4in).
Note: Use smaller needles if your sample works out bigger than this; use bigger needles if your sample works out smaller.

METHOD

Start with the sole.
Using 3mm (UK 11, US 3) knitting needles and black yarn, cast on 27 (31, 35) sts.
Work 2 rows in garter stitch.
Row 3: K1, inc 1, k12 (14, 16), inc 1, k1, inc 1, k12 (14, 16), inc 1, k1 [31, 35, 39 sts].
Repeat these increases on every second row 3 (3, 4) more times, working 2 more stitches each time between the 2nd and 3rd increases [43, 47, 55) sts].
Work 7 (7, 9) rows on these stitches.

INSTEP

K20 (22, 26), sl2, k1, p2sso, k20 (22, 26).
Repeat this double decrease every second row 6 (6, 8) times, knitting one stitch less on each side each time [29 (33, 37) sts].

CUFF

Change to white yarn and work in stocking stitch, decreasing 1 st on the first row [28 (32, 36) sts].
When the cuff measures 3cm (1¼in), i.e. 10 rows, work 1 row of knit on the purl side to mark the fold.
Work a further 9 rows in reverse stocking stitch and cast off.

FINISHING

Sew up the bootie, allowing for a 3cm (1¼in) turn-down cuff.
Using Swiss darning (duplicate stitch), embroider the cuff in black (over the knit sts on what is the right side when the cuff is turned down) following the chart.
Make a second bootie to match.

EMBROIDERY PATTERN

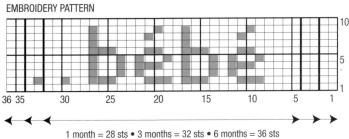

1 month = 28 sts • 3 months = 32 sts • 6 months = 36 sts

☐ 1 st white

▨ 1 st black

Black and White

SIZES

1 month • 3 months • 6 months (instructions for the two larger sizes are given in brackets)

MATERIALS

1 ball each of Bergère de France Idéal (or similar easy-care double knitting yarn) in Truffle (black) and Everest (white) • 3mm (UK 11; US 3) knitting needles

STITCHES

Double decrease, centred (sl2, k1, p2sso): See page 154.
Garter stitch: Knit every row.
Increase 1 stitch (inc 1): See page 156.
Reverse stocking stitch: Purl right-side rows, knit wrong-side rows.
Stocking stitch: Knit right-side rows, purl wrong-side rows.

GAUGE

24 sts and 31 rows in stocking stitch on 3mm (UK 11; US 3) knitting needles = 10 × 10cm (4 × 4in).

Note: Use smaller needles if your sample works out bigger than this; use bigger needles if your sample works out smaller.

METHOD

Start with the sole.
Using black yarn, cast on 27 (31, 35) sts.
Work 2 rows in garter stitch.
Row 3: K1, inc 1, k12 (14, 16), inc 1, k1, inc 1, k12 (14, 16), inc 1, k1 [31 (35, 39) sts].
Repeat these increases on every second row 3 (3, 4) more times, working 2 more stitches each time between the 2nd and 3rd increases [43 (47, 55) sts].
Work 7 (7, 9) rows on these stitches.

INSTEP

K20 (22, 26), sl2, k1, p2sso, k20 (22, 26).
Repeat this double decrease every second row 6 (6, 8) times [29 (33, 37) sts].

CUFF

Change to stocking stitch and work 4 rows in white and 2 rows in black.
Change to reverse stocking stitch and work *4 rows in white and 2 rows in black*. Repeat from* to * twice more, then work 2 rows in white and cast off.

FINISHING

Sew up the bootie, allowing for a 3cm (1¼in) turn-down cuff.
Make a second bootie to match.

17 Little Stripes

18 Mini Moccasins

17 Little Stripes

SIZES

1 month • 3 months • 6 months (instructions for the two larger sizes are given in brackets)

MATERIALS

1 ball each of Bergère de France Caline (or similar easy-care baby/fingering yarn) in Culbuto (burgundy), Kitty (fuchsia pink), Couffin (raspberry red) and Lutin (lime green) • 2.5mm (UK 12; US 2) knitting needles • 3 stitch holders

STITCHES

Double decrease, centred (sl2, k1, p2sso): See page 154.
Garter stitch: Knit every row.

GAUGE

27 sts and 54 rows in garter stitch on 2.5mm (UK 12; US 2) knitting needles = 10 × 10cm (4 × 4in).
Note: Use smaller needles if your sample works out bigger than this; use bigger needles if your sample works out smaller.

METHOD

Start at the top.
Using 2.5mm (UK 12; US 2) needles and burgundy (main colour), cast on 25 (29, 33) sts.
Work 4cm (5cm, 6cm)/1½in (2in, 2⅜in) i.e. 23 (27, 33) rows, in garter stitch.

INSTEP

Slip 9 (10, 11) sts at each side on to stitch holders.
Work stripes on the 7 (9, 11) central stitches in garter stitch: *2 rows pink, 2 rows raspberry, 2 rows lime green, 2 rows burgundy*. Repeat this sequence over 12 (14, 16) rows and finish with 2 rows burgundy. Place the stitches on a stitch holder.

SIDES

Next row: Using burgundy yarn, knit the 9 (10, 11) sts from the right-hand holder, pick up and knit 8 (9, 10) sts along the right edge of the instep, knit the 7 (9, 11) central stitches from the holder, pick up and knit 8 (9, 10) sts along the left edge of the instep and then knit the 9 (10, 11) sts from the left-hand holder [41 (47, 53) sts].
Work 10 (12, 14) rows on these stitches.

SOLE

Next row: Using burgundy yarn, k3 (5, 6), sl2, k1, p2sso, k8 (9, 10), sl2, k1, p2sso, k7 (8, 9), sl2, k1, p2sso, k8 (9, 10), sl2, k1, p2sso, k3 (4, 6).
Repeat these decreases once after 4 rows and twice after that every 2 rows, knitting 1 stitch less at the beginning and end of the row and 2 stitches less between each double decrease [9 (15, 21) sts].
Work 1 row on these stitches and cast off on the following row.

FINISHING

Sew up, allowing for a turn-down cuff.
Make a second bootie to match.

Mini Moccasins

SIZES

1 month • 3 months • 6 months (instructions for the two larger sizes are given in brackets)

MATERIALS

1 ball each of Bergère de France Idéal (or similar easy-care double knitting yarn) in Figue (dark purple), Belladone (mid-purple) and Olivine (light green) • 3mm (UK 11; US 3) knitting needles • 2 mauve buttons • 3 stitch holders

STITCHES

Garter stitch: Knit every row.
Grafting: See page 155.

GAUGE

22 sts and 44 rows in garter stitch on 3mm (UK 11; US 3) knitting needles = 10 × 10cm (4 × 4in).
Note: Use smaller needles if your sample works out bigger than this; use bigger needles if your sample works out smaller.

METHOD

Start at the top.
Using mid-purple yarn, cast on 37 (41, 45) sts. Work 3cm (1¼in) or 14 rows in garter-stitch stripes as follows: *2 rows mid-purple, 2 rows green, 2 rows dark purple, 2 rows green*, repeat from * to *.

INSTEP AND SIDES

Slip 12 (14, 16) sts at each side on to holders.
Using dark purple yarn, knit 14 (16, 18) rows on the 13 central stitches for the instep and slip these stitches on to a holder.
Knit the 12 (14, 16) sts from the right-hand holder, pick up and knit 7 (8, 9) sts along the right edge of the instep, knit the 13 central stitched from the holder, pick up and knit 7 (8, 9) sts along the left edge of the instep and then knit the 12 (14, 16) sts from the left-hand holder [51 (57, 63) sts].
Work 12 (14, 16) rows in garter stitch in the established striped pattern, starting with 2 rows of green, and decreasing 1 st at either side of the 13 central stitches in the 1st row [49 (55, 61) sts].
Slip 19 (22, 25) stitches at each side on to holders.

SOLE

Using dark purple yarn, continue working on the 11 central stitches in garter stitch, knitting together the last stitch of each row with the 1st stitch from the adjacent holder. When there are 5 (5, 6) stitches remaining on each side, join them to the 11 stitches of the sole by grafting (see page 155).

FINISHING

Sew up the back and then make a second bootie to match. Sew a button on to the instep of each bootie, using the photographs as a guide to positioning.

19 Red on Red

20 Dancer's Delight

Red on Red

SIZES

6 months • 1 year • 2 years • 4 years (instructions for the three larger sizes are given in brackets)

MATERIALS

1 ball each of Bergère de France Caline (or similar easy-care baby/fingering yarn) in Spiderman (deep red) and Charlotte (bright red) • 2.5mm (UK 12; US 2) and 3mm (UK 11; US 3) knitting needles • Tapestry needle

STITCHES

Double decrease, left-slanted (sl2, k2tog, p2sso): See page 155.
Grafting: See page 155.
Increases (inc 1): See page 156.
K1 p1 rib: *K1, p1*, repeat from * to * to the end of the row.
Stocking stitch: Knit right-side rows, purl wrong-side rows.

GAUGE

27 sts and 36 rows in stocking stitch on 3mm (UK 11; US 3) knitting needles = 10 × 10cm (4 × 4in).
Note: Use smaller needles if your sample works out bigger than this; use bigger needles if your sample works out smaller.

METHOD

Start at the top.
Using 2.5mm (UK 12; US 2) needles and bright red yarn, cast on 47 (51, 59, 67) sts.
Work 4 rows in k1 p1 rib.
Change to 3mm (UK 11; US 3) knitting needles and deep red yarn, and work 6 rows in stocking stitch.
Row 7: K22 (24, 28, 32), inc 1, k1, inc 1, k1, inc 1, k1, inc 1, k22 (24, 28, 32) [51 (55, 63 71) sts].
Work 1 (1, 3, 3) row(s) on these stitches.
Next row: K23 (25, 29, 33), *inc 1, k1* five times, inc 1, k23 (25, 29, 33) [57 (61, 69, 77) sts].
Work 1 (1, 3, 3) row(s) on these stitches.
Next row: K24 (26, 30, 34), inc 1, k1, inc 1, k3, inc 1, k1, inc 1, k3, inc 1, k1, inc 1, k24 (26, 30, 34) [63 (67, 75, 83) sts].
Work 5 (5, 7, 7) rows on these stitches.
Next row: K23 (25, 29, 33) sts, *k2tog, k1* five times, k2tog, k23 (25, 29, 33) [57 (61, 69, 77) sts].
Work 1 row on these stitches.
Next row: K22 (24, 28, 32) sts, k2tog, k1, sl2, k1, p2sso, k1, sl2, k1, p2sso, k1, k2tog, k22 (24, 28, 32) [51 (55, 63, 71) sts].
Work 1 row and graft the remaining stitches together (see page 155).

Sew up the back seam.
Make a second bootie to match.

CORD TIES

You will need two cords in bright red, each 38cm (40cm, 42cm 44cm)/15in (15¾in, 16½in, 17¼in) long. To make each cord, cut a length of bright red yarn at least 5 times the desired length of the cord. Fold this yarn in half and knot the ends together. Hook the knotted end on to a fixed point such as a door handle and slip a knitting needle through the loop at the other end. Pull to stretch the yarn and twist very tightly by turning the needle. Then fold the twisted cord in half, allowing the yarn to twist on to itself. Tie a knot in the cord close to each end and then trim off the yarn ends to form tassels (see the photographs).

Using a tapestry needle, thread a cord through each bootie, starting at the centre front and weaving over and under 2 sts at a time. Tie the ends in a neat bow.

Dancer's Delight

SIZES

Newborn/1 month • 3 months • 6 months (instructions for the two larger sizes are given in brackets)

MATERIALS

1 ball of Bergère de France Caline (or similar easy-care baby/fingering yarn) in Kitty (fuchsia pink) • 3mm (UK 11; US 3) knitting needles • 2 stitch holders • 2 buttons

STITCHES

Fancy rib (requires an odd number of stitches):

Row 1 (right side): *P1, k1*, repeat from * to * to the end of the row, finishing with p1.

Row 2: *K1, p1*, repeat from * to * to the end of the row, finishing with k1.

Row 3: Repeat row 1.

Row 4: Knit all stitches.

Row 5: Repeat row 1.

Garter stitch: Knit every row.

K2tog: Knit two stitches together as one (see page 154).

K3tog: As k2tog but knit three stitches together.

GAUGE

27 sts and 36 rows in stocking stitch on 3mm (UK 11; US 3) knitting needles = 10 × 10cm (4 × 4in).

Note: Use smaller needles if your sample works out bigger than this; use bigger needles if your sample works out smaller.

METHOD

Start with the sole.

Cast on 9 (11, 11) sts.

Work 6cm (6.5cm, 7cm)/2⅜in (2½in, 2¾in), i.e. 30 (32, 34) rows, in garter stitch. Slip the stitches on to a stitch holder.

FOOT

Cast on 5 (6, 6) sts, pick up and knit 18 (19, 21) sts along the left side of the sole, knit the 9 (11, 11) sts from the holder, pick up and knit 18 (19, 21) sts along the right side of the sole and then cast on 5 (6, 6) sts [55 (61, 65) sts]. Work 4 rows in fancy rib on these stitches.

Slip 23 (25, 27) sts on each side on to holders and work 4 more rows in fancy rib on the 9 (11, 11) central sts, knitting together the last stitch of each row with the first stitch from the holder.

After the last decrease, knit 1 row (right side) on the 30 (34, 36) sts on the left, then work 1 row across all the stitches [51 (57, 61) sts].

Continue in fancy rib on these stitches, decreasing as follows: rib 2, k3tog, rib 13 (15, 17), k3tog, rib 9 (11, 11), k3tog, rib 13 (15, 17), k3tog, rib 2 [43 (49, 53) sts].

Next row: Knit.

Next row: Decrease as follows: rib 1, p3tog, rib 11 (13, 15), p3tog, rib 7 (9, 9), p3tog, rib 11 (13, 15), p3tog, rib 1 [35 (41, 45) sts].

Work 2 rows on these stitches.

Next row: Cast off 8 (9, 10) sts, slip the next 4 (5, 5) sts on to a holder and then cast off the remaining 23 (27, 30) sts.

STRAP

Return to the 4 (5, 5) sts on the holder and work 24 (26, 28) rows in garter stitch.

Next row: K1, k2tog, yon, k1 (2, 2).

Work 3 more rows in garter stitch and cast off.

Sew on the button.

Make a second bootie, reversing the strap.

For Cold Weather

21 Nordic Beauties

22 Cute Cables

Nordic Beauties

SIZES

Newborn/1 month • 3 months • 6 months (instructions for the two larger sizes are given in brackets)

MATERIALS

1 ball each of Bergère de France Caline (or similar easy-care baby/fingering yarn) in Jerry (mid-grey), Baby (blue), Bouba (chocolate brown) and Porcelaine (cream) • 2.5mm (UK 12; US 2) and 3mm (UK 11; US 3) knitting needles • 3 stitch holders • Tapestry needle

STITCHES

Double decrease, centred (sl2, k1, p2sso): See page 154.
Garter stitch: Knit every row.
Grafting: See page 155.
K1 p1 rib: *K1, p1*, repeat from * to * to the end.
Stocking stitch: Knit right-side rows, purl wrong-side rows.

GAUGE

27 sts and 36 rows in stocking stitch on 3mm (UK 11; US 3) knitting needles = 10 × 10cm (4 × 4in).
Note: Use smaller needles if your sample works out bigger than this; use bigger needles if your sample works out smaller.

METHOD

Using blue yarn and 2.5mm (UK 12; US 2) needles, cast on 37 (41, 45) sts. Work 4cm (1½in), i.e. 20 rows, in k1 p1 rib.
Change to mid-grey yarn and 3mm (UK 11; US 3) needles and work 8 (10, 12) rows in stocking stitch, decreasing 6 sts evenly spaced on the first row [31 (35, 39) sts].

UPPER

Slip 11 (13, 15) sts each side on to holders and work 10 (12, 14) rows stocking stitch on the 9 central stitches. Slip these stitches on to a holder. Knit the 11 (13, 15) sts from the right-hand holder, pick up and knit 10 (11, 12) sts along the right edge of the instep, knit the 9 central stitches from the holder, pick up and knit 10 (11, 12) sts along the left edge of the instep and then knit the 11 (13, 15) sts from the left-hand holder [51 (57, 63) sts].
Work 8 (10, 12) rows of stocking stitch on these stitches.

SOLE

Still on 3mm (UK 11; US 3) needles, change to blue yarn and work in garter stitch, decreasing on the first row as follows: k4 (5, 5), sl2, k1, p2sso, k11 (13, 15), sl2, k1, p2sso, k9 (10, 11), sl2, k1, p2sso, k11 (13, 15), sl2, k1, p2sso, k4 (4, 5).
Repeat these decreases on the 4th row and then every 2nd row twice, working 1 stitch less at the beginning and end of the row and 2 sts less between the double decreases each time.
Work 2 rows on the remaining stitches and graft them together.

FINISHING

Embroider the cross-stitch pattern following the chart and using chocolate brown and cream yarns.
Sew up the bootie, allowing for a turn-down cuff.
Work blanket stitch around the edge of the cuff in brown, spacing the stitches 2 stitches apart.
Make a second bootie to match.

CROSS-STITCH EMBROIDERY CHART

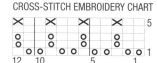

☐ 1 st stocking stitch in mid-grey
○ 1 cross stitch in chocolate brown
✕ 1 cross stitch in cream

Cute Cables

SIZES

1 month/3 months • 6 months (instructions for the larger size are given in brackets)

MATERIALS

1 ball of Bergère de France Idéal (or similar easy-care double knitting yarn) in Vannerie (dark cream) • 3mm (UK 11; US 3) and 3.5mm (UK 9; US 4) knitting needles • Cable needle • 3 stitch holders

STITCHES

Cable (requires a multiple of 6 sts + 2sts):

Row 1 (right side): P2, *k4, p2*, repeat from * to * to end of row.

Row 2 and all even-numbered rows: K2, *p4, k2*, repeat from * to * to end of row.

Row 3: Repeat row 1.

Row 5: P2, *slip 2 sts on to cable needle and leave at front of work. Knit the next 2 sts, then knit the 2 sts from the cable needle, p2*, repeat from * to *.

Rows 7, 9 and 11: Repeat row 1.

Row 13: Start again from row 5.

Garter stitch: Knit every row.

Grafting: See page 155.

Stocking stitch: Knit right-side rows, purl wrong-side rows.

GAUGE

24 sts and 31 rows in stocking stitch on 3mm (UK 11; US 3) knitting needles = 10 × 10cm (4 × 4in).

Note: Use smaller needles if your sample works out bigger than this; use bigger needles if your sample works out smaller.

... Cute Cables

METHOD

Start at the top.

Using 3.5mm (UK 9; US 4) needles, cast on 38 (44) sts.

Work 5cm (6cm)/2in (2⅜in), i.e. 16 (20) rows, in cable pattern.

INSTEP

Change to 3mm (UK 11; US 3) needles. Slip 14 (17) sts at each side on to holders. Work 10 (12) rows stocking stitch on the 10 central stitches. Slip these stitches on to a holder.

FOOT

Knit the 14 (17) sts from the right-hand holder, pick up and knit 8 (9) sts along the right edge of the instep, knit the 10 central stitches from the holder, pick up and knit 8 (9) sts along the left side of the instep and knit the 14 (17) sts from the left-hand holder. Change to garter stitch.

Next row: Decrease 2 sts evenly across the group of 14 (17) sts at each side [50 (58) sts]. Work 5 (7) more rows on these stitches.

SOLE

Slip 20 (24) sts each side on to holders. Work in garter stitch using the 3mm (UK 11; US 3) needles on the 10 central stitches, knitting together the last stitch of each row with the first stitch on the adjacent holder until 5 sts remain on each side.

FINISHING

Graft the remaining stitches from the holder to the stitches of the sole (see page 155).

Sew up the back seam.

Make a second bootie to match.

TIP

If you have never tried cabling before, this is an ideal first project because it is an extremely simple cable pattern and the booties are small and quick to make. Once you have tried these, you will want to try some of the other cable patterns in this book.

CABLE CHART

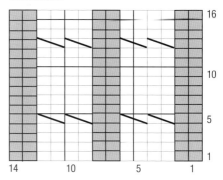

	1 knit st on right side (purl on wrong side)
	1 purl st on right side (knit on wrong side)
	Cable

23 Pixie Boots

23 Pixie Boots

SIZES

Newborn • 1 month • 3 months • 6 months (instructions for the three larger sizes are given in brackets)

MATERIALS

1 ball of Bergère de France Jaspée (or similar easy-care double knitting or light aran-weight yarn) in Pangolin (speckled brown) • 1 ball of Bergère de France Berlaine (or similar double-knitting yarn) in Bisque (hot orange) • 3.5mm (UK 9; US 4) and 4mm (UK8; US 6) knitting needles • 3 stitch holders • Pompom maker • Tapestry needle

STITCHES

Grafting: See page 155.
Increases: See page 156.
K1 p1 rib: *K1, p1* repeat from * to * end.
Stocking stitch: Knit right-side rows, purl wrong-side rows.

GAUGE

19 sts and 26 rows in stocking stitch on 4mm (UK8; US 6) knitting needles = 10 × 10cm (4 × 4in).
Note: Use smaller needles if your sample works out bigger than this; use bigger needles if your sample works out smaller.

METHOD

Using 3.5mm (UK 9; US 4) needles and the brown yarn, cast on 23 (25, 27, 29) sts and work 5cm (2in), i.e. 14 rows, in k1 p1 rib.

UPPER

Change to 4mm (UK8; US 6) and work in stocking stitch, increasing 1 st at the beginning of the 1st row [24 (26, 28, 30) sts].
When work measures 6cm (6cm, 7cm, 8cm)/2⅜in (2⅜in, 2¾in, 3¼in), i.e. 16 (16, 18, 20) rows), slip 8 (9, 10, 11) sts on each side on to a holder and work 6 (8, 10, 12) rows of stocking stitch on the 8 central stitches. Slip these stitches on to a holder.

SIDES

Still using the 4mm (UK8; US 6) needles, knit the 8 (9, 10, 11) sts from the right-hand holder, pick up and knit 5 (7, 9, 11) sts along the right edge of the instep, knit the 8 central stitches from the holder, pick up and knit 5 (7, 9, 11) sts along the left side of the instep and then knit the 8 (9, 10, 11) sts from the left-hand holder [34 (40, 46, 52) sts].
Work 3 (3, 5, 5) rows in stocking stitch on these stitches.

SOLE

Slip 13 (16, 19, 22) sts each side on to holders. Work in garter stitch on the 8 central stitches, knitting together the last stitch of each row with the first stitch on the adjacent holder until 4 sts remain on each side. Graft the remaining stitches from the holders to the stitches of the sole (see page 155).

FINISHING

Sew up the back seam, allowing for a 2.5cm (1in) turn-down cuff.
Make a second bootie to match.
Make a 3cm (1¼in) diameter pompom in hot orange for each bootie and attach it to the top of the instep (see the photographs).
Embroider a line of running stitch in hot orange all round each bootie, one row up from the sole.

Little Indian

SIZES

6 months • 1 year • 2 years (instructions for the two larger sizes are given in brackets)

MATERIALS

1 ball each of Bergère de France Alaska (or similar easy-care aran yarn) in Agneau (cream), Rapace (dark brown) and Perdrix (partridge grey) • 1 ball each of Bergère de France Magic (or similar easy-care chunky yarn) in Brique (brick red) and Corail (coral) • 4.5mm (UK 7; US 7) and 5.5mm (UK 5; US 9) knitting needles • 3 stitch holders • Tapestry needle

STITCHES

Grafting: See page 155.
K1 p1 rib: *K1, p1*, repeat from * to * to the end.
Stocking stitch: Knit right-side rows, purl wrong-side rows.

GAUGE

15 sts and 20 rows in stocking stitch on 5.5mm (UK 5; US 9) knitting needles = 10 × 10cm (4 × 4in).
Note: Use smaller needles if your sample works out bigger than this; use bigger needles if your sample works out smaller.

METHOD

Start at the top.
Using 4.5mm (UK 7; US 7) needles and cream yarn, cast on 23 (25, 27) sts and work 6 (8, 8) rows in k1 p1 rib. Change to dark-brown yarn and work another 6 (8, 8) rows in k1 p1 rib.

Change to 5.5mm (UK 5; US 9) needles and work in stocking stitch. Work 1 row in dark brown, then change to partridge grey and work 3 (3, 5) rows in stocking stitch.

INSTEP AND SIDES

Slip 7 (8, 9) stitches at each side on to holders. Work 4 (6, 8) rows in stocking stitch on the 9 central stitches and slip these stitches on to a holder.
Knit the 7 (8, 9) sts from the right-hand holder, pick up and knit 4 (5, 6) sts along the right edge of the instep, knit the 9 central stitches from the holder, pick up and knit 4 (5, 6) sts along the left side of the instep and then knit the 7 (8, 9) sts from the left-hand holder [31 (35, 39) sts].
Work 4 (4, 6) rows in stocking stitch on these stitches.

SOLE

Slip 11 (13, 15) stitches at each side on to holders.
Change to dark brown yarn and work in stocking stitch on the 9 central stitches, knitting together the last stitch of the sole and the first stitch from the holder on each row.
When 5 stitches remain on the holders, graft the remaining stitches to the 7 (8, 9) sts of the sole.

FINISHING

Embroider crosses above the second row of the bootie sides, alternating brick red and coral yarns (see chart).
Sew up the back seam, allowing for a 3cm (1¼in) turn-down cuff.
Make six tassels, each from three strands of dark-brown yarn, and knot them round the edge of the cuff.
Make a second bootie to match.

TIP

You only need small amounts of the brick red and coral yarns, so see if you have any suitable yarns in your stash rather than buying whole balls specifically for this project. Alternatively, you could use tapestry yarn or embroidery thread.

EMBROIDERY CHART

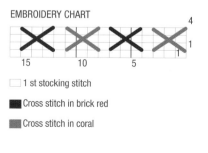

☐ 1 st stocking stitch

■ Cross stitch in brick red

■ Cross stitch in coral

25 Ankle Boots

26 Softly Softly

Ankle Boots

SIZES

Newborn/1 month • 3 months • 6 months • 1 year (instructions for the three larger sizes are given in brackets)

MATERIALS

1 ball of Bergère de France Teddy (fluffy novelty yarn) in Nounours (teddy brown) • 1 ball of Bergère de France Idéal (or similar easy-care double knitting yarn) in Meije (cream) • 5mm (UK 6; US 8) knitting needles • 3mm (UK 11; US D/3) crochet hook for making the cord ties

STITCHES

Garter stitch: Knit every row.
Increase (inc 1): See page 156.
K3tog: Knit three stitches together as one. This reduces the stitch count by two.
Stocking stitch: Knit right-side rows, purl wrong-side rows.

GAUGE

14 sts and 23 rows in stocking stitch on 5mm (UK 6; US 8) knitting needles = 10 × 10cm (4 × 4in).
Note: Use smaller needles if your sample works out bigger than this; use bigger needles if your sample works out smaller.

METHOD

Start with the sole.

Using 5mm (UK 6; US 8) needles and the camel-coloured yarn, cast on 15 (17, 19, 21) sts.

Row 1: K1, inc 1, k6 (7, 8, 9), inc 1, k1, inc 1, k6 (7, 8, 9), inc 1, k1 [19 (21, 23, 25) sts].

Continue in garter stitch, repeat these increases on the next 2 rows, working 1 st more at the beginning and end and 2 sts more between the 2nd and 3rd increases [27 (29, 31, 33) sts].

Work 6 more rows without increasing on these stitches.

INSTEP AND ANKLE

Row 1: K12 (13, 14, 15) sts, k3tog, k12 (13, 14, 15).

Repeat this decrease every second row twice more [21 (23, 25, 27) sts].

Work 6 (6, 6, 8) rows stocking stitch on these stitches and cast off.

Sew up the back of the bootie.

Make a second bootie to match.

CORD TIES

Using a 3mm (UK 11; US D/3) crochet hook and cream yarn, make a chain 45cm (18in) long. Work 1 slip stitch into each stitch of the chain and fasten off. Repeat for the second bootie.

Thread the chain between the stitches of the ankle and tie in a bow in front.

TIP

Use garter stitch instead of stocking stitch to show off the fluffy texture of the yarn.

Softly Softly

SIZES

3 months • 6 months (instructions for the larger size are given in brackets)

MATERIALS

1 ball of Bergère de France Teddy (fluffy novelty yarn) in Blanche-Neige (snow white) • 4mm (UK8; US 6) knitting needles • Stitch holder • 2 tiny white buttons

STITCHES

Garter stitch: Knit every row.
K2tog: Knit two stitches together as one. This reduces the stitch count by one.
Single decrease, right slanted (k2tog): See page 154.

TENSION

16 sts and 25 rows in garter stitch on 4mm (UK8; US 6) knitting needles = 10 × 10cm (4 × 4in).
Note: Use smaller needles if your sample works out bigger than this; use bigger needles if your sample works out smaller.

METHOD

Start with the sole.
Cast on 7 sts. Work 6cm (7cm)/2⅜in (2¾in), i.e. 16 (20) rows, in garter stitch and leave the stitches on a stitch holder.

FOOT

Cast on 3 sts, pick up and knit 11 (13) sts along the long side of the sole, knit the 7 stitches of the sole from the holder, pick up and knit 11 (13) sts along the other long side and then cast on 3 sts [35 (39) sts].
Work 10 rows in garter stitch on these stitches.
Now work short-row shaping as follows: K20 (22), k2tog, turn, k6, k2tog, turn, k6, k2tog, turn, and continue in this way until 27 (29) sts remain. Knit to the end of the row and cast off.

STRAP

Cast on 14 (16) sts. Knit 1 row and then cast off all stitches.

FINISHING

Sew up the back seam. Sew the strap on one side and the button on the other. Pull one stitch of the strap aside to form the buttonhole.
Make a second slipper to match, but sew the strap and button on the opposite sides.

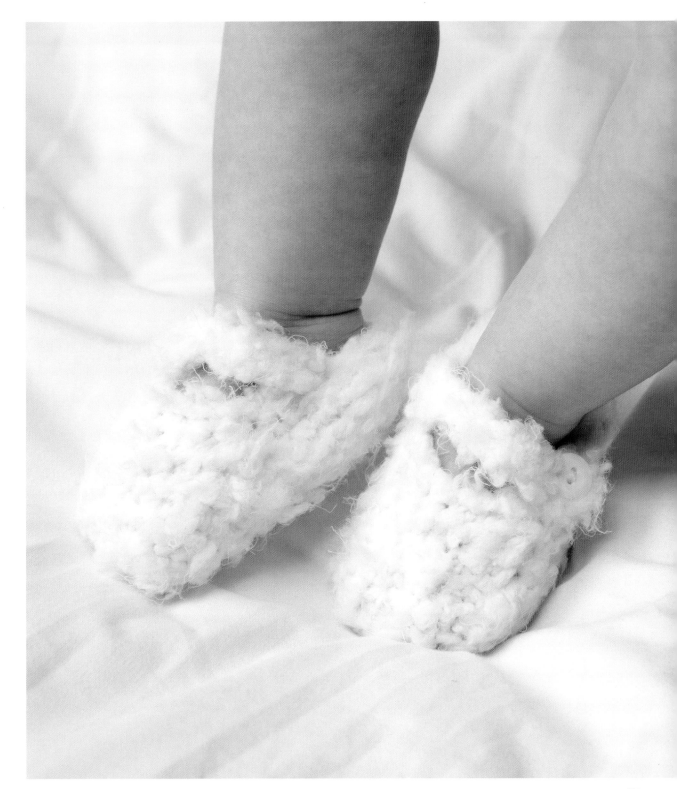

27 Puppy Dogs

28 Baby Bears

27 Puppy Dogs

SIZES

Newborn/1 month • 3 months • 6 months (instructions for the two larger sizes are given in brackets)

MATERIALS

1 ball each of Bergère de France Caline (or similar easy-care baby/fingering yarn) in Jerry (mid-grey), Bouba (chocolate brown) and Porcelaine (cream) • 2.5mm (UK 12; US 2) and 3mm (UK 11; US 3) knitting needles • 3 stitch holders • Tapestry needle

STITCHES

Double decrease, centred (sl2, k1, p2sso): See page 154.

Garter stitch: Knit every row.

Grafting: See page 155.

K1 p1 rib: *K1, p1* repeat from * to * to the end.

K3tog: Knit three stitches together as one. This reduces the stitch count by two.

Single increase or decrease: See pages 154–156.

Stocking stitch: Knit right-side rows, purl wrong-side rows.

Swiss darning (duplicate stitch): See page 154.

GAUGE

27 sts and 36 rows in stocking stitch on 3mm (UK 11; US 3) knitting needles = 10 × 10cm (4 × 4in).

Note: Use smaller needles if your sample works out bigger than this; use bigger needles if your sample works out smaller.

METHOD

Using 2.5mm (UK 12; US 2) knitting needles and mid-grey yarn, cast on 37 (41, 45) sts. Work 4cm (1½in), i.e. 18 rows, in k1 p1 rib.

Next row: Decrease 6 stitches evenly across the row by working k3tog three times at even spacing [31 (35, 39) sts].

Continue in k1 p1 rib until work measures 6cm (7cm, 7.5cm)/2⅜in (2¾in, 3in), which is 26 (30, 32) rows.

UPPER

Slip 11 (13, 15) sts each side on to stitch holders, change to 3mm (UK 11; US 3) needles and cream yarn, and work 10 (12, 14) rows in stocking stitch on the 9 central stitches. Slip these stitches on to a stitch holder.

SIDES

Knit the 11 (13, 15) sts from the right-hand holder, pick up and knit 10 (11, 12) sts along the right edge of the instep, knit the 9 stitches from the central holder, pick up and knit 10 (11, 12) sts along the left side of the instep and then knit the 11 (13, 15) sts from the left-hand holder [51 (57, 63) sts].

Change to 2.5mm (UK 12; US 2) needles and mid-grey yarn, and work 8 (10, 12) rows in k1 p1 rib on these stitches.

SOLE

Slip 21 (24, 27) sts on each side on to holders. Change to garter stitch and work on the 9 central stitches, knitting together the last stitch of the sole and the first stitch from the holder on each row.

When 5 stitches remain on the holders, graft the remaining stitches to the 9 sts of the sole (see page 155).

DOG'S FACE

Thread a tapestry needle with a short length of yarn and embroider the dog's face on the instep, following the chart and using Swiss darning (duplicate stitch) unless otherwise specified.

Now make two ears as follows:

Using 3mm (UK 11; US 3) needles and brown yarn, cast on 3 sts. Work in stocking stitch, increasing 1 st each side, 1 stitch from the edge, on alternate rows twice, then decrease 1 st each side 1 stitch from the edge. Work 1 row on the remaining 5 sts.

Next row: k1, sl2, k1, p2sso, k1. Cast off the remaining 3 sts.

Sew the ears to the top of the instep, using the photographs as your guide to positioning.

FINISHING

Sew up the back seam, allowing for a turn-down cuff of 2cm (¾in).
Make a second bootie to match.

TIP

Can't decide whether to make the dog or the bear slippers? If you buy one ball in each of the three colours – mid-grey, chocolate brown, and cream – you will have enough to make both pairs. Problem solved.

EMBROIDERY CHART

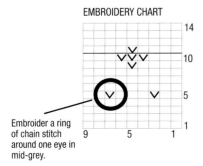

Embroider a ring of chain stitch around one eye in mid-grey.

☑ 1 st in cream yarn (Swiss darning)

Baby Bears

SIZES

Newborn/1 month • 3 months • 6 months (instructions for the two larger sizes are given in brackets)

MATERIALS

1 ball of Bergère de France Caline (or similar easy-care baby/fingering yarn) in Bouba (chocolate brown), Jerry (mid-grey) and Porcelaine (cream) • 2.5mm (UK 12; US 2) and 3mm (UK 11; US 3) knitting needles • 3 stitch holders • Tapestry needle

STITCHES

Garter stitch: Knit every row.
Grafting: See page 155.
K3tog: Knit three stitches together as one. This reduces the stitch count by two.
Stocking stitch: Knit right-side rows, purl wrong-side rows.
Swiss darning (duplicate stitch): See page 154.

GAUGE

27 sts and 36 rows in stocking stitch on 3mm (UK 11; US 3) knitting needles = 10 × 10cm (4 × 4in).
Note: Use smaller needles if your sample works out bigger than this; use bigger needles if your sample works out smaller.

METHOD

Using 2.5mm (UK 12; US 2) needles and brown yarn, cast on 37 (41, 45) sts. Work 3.5cm (4cm, 4.5cm)/1⅜in (1½in, 1¾in), i.e. 22 (24, 26) rows, in garter stitch.
Next row: Decrease 6 stitches evenly across the row [31 (35, 39) sts].
Continue working in garter stitch for a further 3cm (3cm, 3.5cm)/1¼in (1¼in, 1⅜in), i.e. 14 (16, 18) rows.

UPPER

When work measures 6.5cm (7cm, 7.5cm)/2½in (2¾in, 3in), i.e. 36 (40, 44) rows, slip 11 (13, 15) sts each side on to a stitch holder, change to mid-grey yarn and the 3mm (UK 11; US 3) needles and work 12 (14, 16) rows in stocking stitch on the 9 central stitches. Slip these stitches on to a holder.

SIDES

Knit the 11 (13, 15) sts from the right-hand holder, pick up and knit 10 (11, 12) sts along the right edge of the instep, knit the 9 central stitches from the holder, pick up and knit 10 (11, 12) sts along the left side of the instep and then knit the 11 (13, 15) sts from the left-hand holder [51 (57, 63) sts].
Change to brown yarn and the 2.5mm (UK 12; US 2) needles and work 10 (12, 14) rows in garter stitch on these stitches.

SOLE

Slip 21 (24, 27) sts on each side on to holders. Continue in garter stitch on 2.5mm (UK 12; US 2) needles and work on the 9 central stitches, knitting together the last stitch of the sole and the first stitch from the adjacent holder on each row.
When 5 stitches remain on the holders, graft the remaining stitches to the 9 sts of the sole (see page 155).

BEAR'S FACE

Thread a tapestry needle with a short length of yarn and embroider the instep, following the chart and using Swiss darning (duplicate stitch) for the muzzle, satin stitch for the nose and backstitch for the mouth.
Now make two ears as follows:
Using 2.5mm (UK 12; US 2) needles and cream yarn, cast on 5 sts. Work 4 rows in garter stitch.
Row 5: K1, k3tog, k1. Cast off.
Sew the ears to the top of the instep, using the photographs as a guide.

FINISHING

Sew up the back seam, allowing for a turn-down cuff of 2.5cm (3cm, 3.5cm)/1in (1¼in, 1⅜in).
Make a second bootie to match.

EMBROIDERY CHART

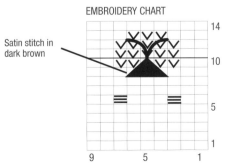

Satin stitch in
dark brown

14

10

5

1

9   5   1

≡ Dark brown

☑ 1 duplicate st in cream

29 Woolly Gaiters

30 Little Legwarmers

Woolly Gaiters

SIZES

3 months • 6 months • 1 year (instructions for the two larger sizes are given in brackets)

MATERIALS

1 ball of Bergère de France Sport (or similar worsted-weight wool-mix yarn) in Kraft (warm brown) • 4.5mm (UK 7; US 7) knitting needles

STITCHES

Garter stitch: Knit every row.

GAUGE

18 sts and 35 rows in garter stitch using 4.5mm (UK 7; US 7) knitting needles = 10 × 10cm (4 × 4in).

Note: Use smaller needles if your sample works out bigger than this; use bigger needles if your sample works out smaller.

METHOD

Cast on 31 (33, 35) sts.

Work 10cm (11cm, 12cm)/4in (4¼in, 4¾in), i.e. 36 (40, 44) rows, in garter stitch.

Cast off.

STRAP

Cast on 14 (15, 16) sts, and work 3 rows in garter stitch.

Cast off.

FINISHING

Fold the gaiter in half and sew up the side.

Little Legwarmers

SIZES

3 months • 6 months • 1 year • 2 years (instructions for the three larger sizes are given in brackets)

MATERIALS

1 ball of Bergère de France Berlaine (or similar worsted-weight woollen yarn) in Albâtre (cream) • 3mm (UK 11; US 3) and 3.5mm (UK 9; US 4) knitting needles

STITCHES

Bobble: k1, yon, k1 into same stitch, turn, p3, turn, sl1, k1, psso.
Double decrease, centred (sl2, k1, p2sso): See page 154.
K3 p3 rib: *K3, p3*, repeat from * to * to the end.
Pattern panel: Refer to the chart.
Reverse stocking stitch: Purl right-side rows, knit wrong-side rows.
Single decrease, left slanted (sl1, k1, psso): See page 154.
Single decrease, right slanted (k2tog): See page 154.

GAUGE

22 sts and 28 rounds in stocking stitch on 3.5mm (UK 9; US 4) knitting needles = 10 × 10cm (4 × 4in).

Note: Use smaller needles if your sample works out bigger than this; use bigger needles if your sample works out smaller.

METHOD

Using 3mm (UK 11; US 3) needles, cast on 31 (35, 39, 43) sts.
Work 4 rows in k3 p3 rib, starting the row with k2 (4, 3, 2) and continuing *p3, k3*, repeat from * to *.
Change to 3.5mm (UK 9; US 4) needles and work as follows: work 9 (11, 13, 15) sts in reverse stocking stitch, work 13 sts in pattern from the chart then work 9 (11, 13, 15) sts in reverse stocking stitch. The first row of the reverse stocking stitch will be a purl row.
When work measures 7cm (7cm, 8cm 9cm)/2¾in (2¾in, 3¼in, 3½in), i.e. 26 (26, 30, 34) rows, change to 3mm (UK 11; US 3) needles, work 4 rows in k3 p3 rib and cast off.

FINISHING

Fold the leg warmer in half with right sides facing and sew up the seam. Make a second legwarmer to match.

Sew one end of the strap to the end of the seam and the other end to the bottom edge at the fold.
Make a second gaiter to match.

PANEL PATTERN

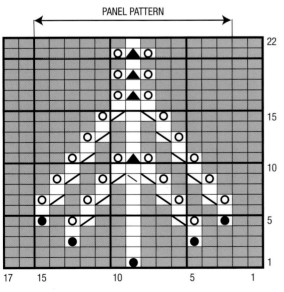

▨ 1 st reverse stocking stitch		◿ 1 single decrease (sl1, k1, psso)	
☐ K1 on right side, p1 on wrong side		◉ K2tog	
◉ 1 bobble		▲ Yon	
		☐ Sl1, k2tog, psso	

For Warm Weather

31 Summer Sandals

32 Retro Slippers

Summer Sandals

SIZES

3 months • 6 months (instructions for the larger size are given in brackets)

MATERIALS

1 ball of Bergère de France Coton Fifty (or similar fine cotton-mix yarn) in Mûrier (deep pink) and small amounts in Lobelia (pink) and Herbage (olive green) • 3mm (UK 11; US 3) and 3.5mm (UK 9; US 4) knitting needles • 3 stitch holders • 2 small mauve buttons

STITCHES

Double decrease, centred (sl2, k1, p2sso): See page 154.
Garter stitch: Knit every row.
Grafting: See page 155.
Single decrease, right slanted (k2tog): See page 154.
Stocking stitch: Knit right-side rows, purl wrong-side rows.

GAUGE

26 sts and 37 rows in stocking stitch on 3mm (UK 11; US 3) knitting needles = 10 × 10cm (4 × 4in).

Note: Use smaller needles if your sample works out bigger than this; use bigger needles if your sample works out smaller.

METHOD

Begin at the top.

Using 3mm (UK 11; US 3) knitting needles and deep pink yarn, cast on 14 (15) sts. Work 2 rows in stocking stitch, 2 rows in garter stitch and then 4 rows in stocking stitch. Slip the stitches on to a stitch holder.

Using 3mm (UK 11; US 3) knitting needles and deep pink yarn, cast on 30 (32) sts. Work 1 row of stocking stitch.

Row 2: Make a buttonhole by working k2tog, yon, 2 stitches in from the left edge.

Work 1 row of stocking stitch.

Row 4: Cast off 16 (17) sts at the left side. Work 8 more rows on the remaining 14 (15) sts. Slip these stitches on to a stitch holder.

INSTEP

Using 3.5mm (UK 9; US 4) needles, cast on 9 (11) sts and work 8 rows in stocking stitch. Slip these stitches on to a stitch holder.

Knit the 14 (15) sts from the holder with the buttonhole band, cast on 5 sts, pick up and knit 5 (6) sts along the right edge of the instep, knit the 9 (11) sts from the holder, pick up and knit 5 (6) sts along the left edge of the instep, cast on 5 sts and then knit the 14 (15) sts from the holder without the buttonhole [57 (63) sts]. Work 10 rows stocking stitch on these stitches.

SOLE

Change to 3mm (UK 11; US 3) needles and garter stitch, and decrease as follows: k4 (5), sl2, k1, p2sso, k14 (15), sl2, k1, p2sso, k9 (11), sl2, k1, p2sso, k14 (15), sl2, k1, p2sso, k4 (5).

Repeat these decreases so they come one above the other on every second row 3 (4) times more. Work 2 rows on the remaining 41 (43) stitches and graft the remaining stitches together (see page 155).

LOOP

Pick up 4 stitches from the 3 central stitches of the instep. Work 14 rows in stocking stitch and cast off.

FINISHING

Sew up the back seam. Fold the loop in half and stitch down, then pass the strap through the loop.

Embroider the instep with cross stitch in pink and olive green, following the chart.

Sew on the button to correspond with the buttonhole.

Make a second sandal with the button and buttonhole on the opposite side.

TIP

You only need tiny amounts of the pink and olive-green yarns so you will have lots leftover. You could use the leftover yarns to make another pair of booties, such as the Retro Slippers that follow. Another idea is to work the cross-stitch pattern in embroidery cotton.

EMBROIDERY CHART

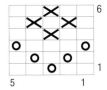

✕ 1 cross stitch in pink

○ 1 cross stitch in olive green

 # Retro Slippers

SIZES

Newborn • 1 month • 3 months • 6 months (instructions for the three larger sizes are given in brackets)

MATERIALS

1 ball of Bergère de France Coton Fifty (or similar fine cotton-mix yarn) in Lobelia (pink) and small amount in Mûrier (deep pink) • 2.5mm (UK 12; US 2) needles • Stitch holder • Tapestry needle

STITCHES

Garter stitch: Knit every row.
Single decrease, left slanted (sl1, k1, psso): See page 155.
Single decrease, right slanted (k2tog): See page 154.

GAUGE

27 sts and 54 rows in garter stitch on 2.5mm (UK 12; US 2) knitting needles = 10 × 10cm (4 × 4in).

Note: Use smaller needles if your sample works out bigger than this; use bigger needles if your sample works out smaller.

METHOD

Start with the sole.

Using pink yarn, cast on 14 sts. Work 5.5cm (6cm, 6.5cm, 7cm)/2¼in (2⅜in, 2½in, 2¾in), i.e. 34 (36, 38, 40) rows, in garter stitch and slip these stitches on to a stitch holder.

FOOT

Using pink yarn, cast on 6 sts, pick up and knit 15 (16, 17, 18) sts along the right edge of the sole, knit the 14 sts from the holder, pick up and knit 15 (16, 17, 18) sts along the left edge of the sole and then cast on 6 sts [56 (58, 60, 62) sts]. Work 14 (14, 16, 16) rows in garter stitch on these stitches.

INSTEP

K33 (34, 35, 36), sl1, k1, psso; turn.
Next row: K11, k2tog and turn.

Next row: K11, sl1, k1, psso and turn.

Repeat these 2 rows until there are only 16 (17, 18, 19) sts remaining on each side.

After the last decrease, turn and knit the 12 stitches of the instep and place the 16 (17, 18, 19) sts on the left on a holder.

Next row: K1, *k2tog, k6*, repeat from * to * and finish with k1 (3, 5, 7).

Cast off the remaining stitches

FINISHING

Sew up the back seam and then join the sole to the 6 stitches cast on at each side of the foot.

Make a second slipper to match.

Make two 30cm (12in) cords in deep pink, following the instructions on page 54. Using a tapestry needle, thread the cord through the knitted slippers, one row below the top of each slipper and starting 2cm (¾in) from the back seam. Tie in a bow at the back.

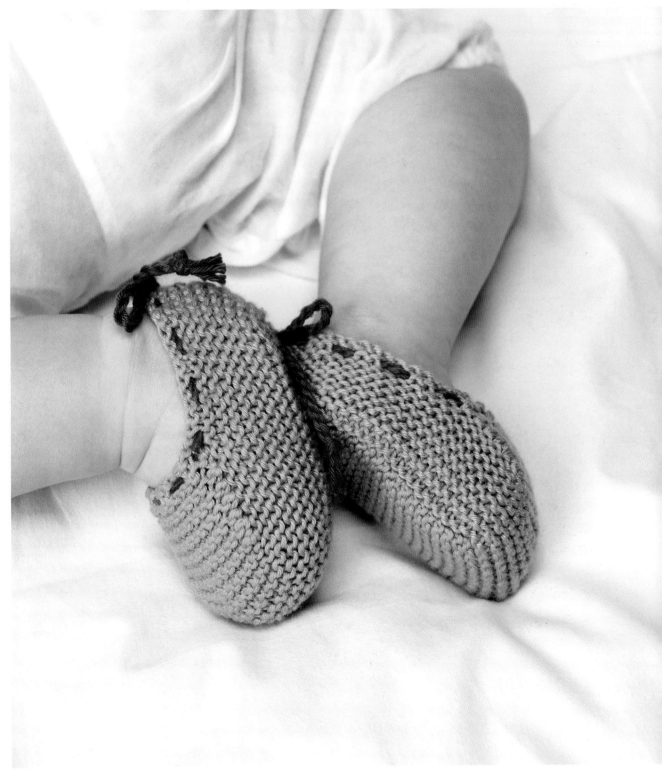

33 Espadrilles

34 Top Trainers

Espadrilles

SIZES

1 month • 3 months • 6 months (instructions for the two larger sizes are given in brackets)

MATERIALS

1 ball each of Bergère de France Bergerine (or similar cotton-wool mix yarn) in Etang (mid-blue) and Rotin (mid-brown) plus a small amount of Berbère (cream)
• 3mm (UK 11; US 3) and 3.5mm (UK 9; US 4) knitting needles • Stitch holder
• Tapestry needle

STITCHES

Garter stitch: Knit every row.
Single decrease, left slanted (sl1, k1, psso): See page 154.
Single decrease, right slanted (k2tog): See page 154.
Stocking stitch: Knit right-side rows, purl wrong-side rows.

GAUGE

21 sts and 28 rows in stocking stitch on 3.5mm (UK 9; US 4) knitting needles = 10 × 10cm (4 × 4in).
Note: Use smaller needles if your sample works out bigger than this; use bigger needles if your sample works out smaller.

METHOD

Start with the sole.
Using 3.5mm (UK 9; US 4) knitting needles and mid-blue yarn, cast on 9 (10, 11) sts. Work 6cm (6.5cm, 7cm)/2⅜in (2½in, 2¾in), i.e. 18 (20, 22) rows, in stocking stitch and slip these stitches on to a stitch holder.

FOOT

Using 3.5mm (UK 9; US 4) knitting needles, cast on 5 (5, 6) sts, pick up 11 (13, 14) sts along the right edge of the sole, knit the 9 (10, 11) sts from the holder, pick up 11 (13, 14) sts along the left edge of the sole and then cast on 5 (5, 6) sts [41 (46, 51) sts].
Change to 3mm (UK 11; US 3) needles and mid-brown yarn and work 4 rows of garter stitch on these stitches.
Change back to 3.5mm (UK 9; US 4) needles and mid-blue yarn and work 8 (8, 10) rows of stocking stitch.

INSTEP

K24 (27, 30), sl1, k1, psso; turn.
Next row: K8 (9, 10), k2tog; turn.
Next row: K8 (9, 10), sl1, k1, psso; turn.
Repeat these 2 rows until there are only 9 (10, 11) sts remaining on each side. After the last decrease, turn and knit the 8 (9, 10) stitches of the instep. Place these stitches on a holder.
Return to the 9 (10, 11) sts on the left. Using 3mm (UK 11; US 3) needles and mid-brown yarn, work 1 row in garter stitch and cast off knitwise on the next row.
Do the same with the 9 (10, 11) sts on the right.
Pick up and knit 5 (6, 7) sts along the side of the bootie, knit the 8 (9, 10) central sts from the holder and then pick up and knit 5 (6, 7) sts along the other side of the bootie. Change to 3mm (UK 11; US 3) needles and, using mid-brown yarn, work 1 row in garter stitch. Cast off knitwise on the next row.

FINISHING

Sew up the back seam and then join the sole to the 5 (5, 6) stitches cast on at each side of the foot.
Thread the tapestry needle with cream yarn and work blanket stitch across the two rows of mid-brown garter stitch around the sole, to look like espadrilles.
Make a second espadrille to match.

34 Top Trainers

SIZES

1 month • 3 months • 6 months (instructions for the two larger sizes are given in brackets)

MATERIALS

1 ball each of Bergère de France Idéal (or similar easy-care double knitting yarn) in Orque (airforce blue) and Meije (cream) • 3mm (UK 11; US 3) knitting needles • 2.5mm (UK 12; US C/2) crochet hook • Stitch holder • Tapestry needle

STITCHES

Garter stitch: Knit every row.
Single decrease, left slanted (sl1, k1, psso): See page 154.
Single decrease, right slanted (k2tog): See page 154.

GAUGE

24 sts and 31 rows in garter stitch on 3mm (UK 11; US 3) knitting needles = 10 × 10cm (4 × 4in).
Note: Use smaller needles if your sample works out bigger than this; use bigger needles if your sample works out smaller.

METHOD

Start with the sole.

Using blue yarn, cast on 12 sts. Work 6cm (6.5cm, 7cm)/2⅜in (2½in, 2¾in), i.e. 28 (32, 36) rows, in garter stitch and slip these stitches on to a stitch holder.

FOOT

Using blue yarn, cast on 5 sts, pick up and knit 14 (16, 18) sts along the right edge of the sole, knit the 12 sts from the stitch holder, pick up 14 (16, 18) sts along the left edge of the sole and then cast on 5 sts [50 (54, 58) sts].
Change to cream yarn and work 4 rows in garter stitch on these stitches.
Change back to blue yarn and work a further 12 (14, 16) rows.

INSTEP

Work short-row shaping as follows:
K29 (31, 33), sl1, k1, psso; turn.
Next row: K9, k2tog; turn.
Next row: k9, sl1, k1, psso and turn.
Repeat these 2 rows until there are only 10 (12, 14) sts remaining on each side.
After the last decrease, turn and knit the 11 stitches of the instep and place the 10 (11, 12) stitches on the left on a holder.
Next row: K2 (4, 3), *k2tog, k6* repeat from * to * and finish with k2 (4, 3).
Cast off the remaining stitches.

FINISHING

Sew up the back seam and then join the sole to the 5 stitches cast on at each side of the foot.
Using cream yarn, crochet a chain of 130 sts and use the tapestry needle to lace it across the instep of the bootie to look like a trainer. Alternatively, you could substitute real ecru laces for the crochet chain.
Use the cream yarn to embroider a row of running stitch one row above the cream garter-stitch around the lower edge of the sides. Work a second row of running stitch one row below the top of the trainer.
Make a second trainer to match.

35 Strawberry
Fair

36 Flower Sandals

35 Strawberry Fair

SIZES

1 month • 3 months • 6 months (instructions for the two larger sizes are given in brackets)

MATERIALS

1 ball each of Bergère de France Coton Fifty (or similar fine cotton-mix yarn) in Bengale (spicy red), Ecarlate (scarlet) and Sauterelle (bright green) plus a small amount of Coco (cream) • 2.5mm (UK 12; US 2) and 3mm (UK 11; US 3) knitting needles • 2.5mm (UK 12; US C/2) crochet hook • 2 stitch holders • 2 press studs • Tapestry needle

STITCHES

Crochet stitches: See pages 152–153.
K1 p1 rib: *K1, p1*, repeat from * to * to the end.
K2tog: Knit two stitches together as one. This reduces the stitch count by one.
Stocking stitch: Knit right-side rows, purl wrong-side rows.

GAUGE

26 sts and 37 rows in stocking stitch on 3mm (UK 11; US 3) knitting needles = 10 × 10cm (4 × 4in).
Note: Use smaller needles if your sample works out bigger than this; use bigger needles if your sample works out smaller.

METHOD

Start with the sole.
Using 3mm (UK 11; US 3) needles and the spicy red yarn, cast on 9 (10, 11) sts. Work 7cm (7.5cm, 8cm) 2¾in (3in, 3¼in), i.e. 24 (26, 28) rows, in stocking stitch and slip the stitches on to a holder.

FOOT

Using 3mm (UK 11; US 3) needles and spicy red yarn, cast on 4 (5, 5) sts, pick up 19 (20, 22) sts along the right edge of the sole, knit the 9 (10, 11) sts from the holder, pick up 19 (20, 22) sts along the left edge of the sole and then cast on 4 (5, 5) sts [55 (60, 65) sts]. Work 3cm (3.5cm, 4cm)/1¼in (1⅜in, 1½in), i.e. 10 (12, 14) rows, in stocking stitch on these stitches.

INSTEP

Slip 17 stitches on each side on to holders. Work 12 (14, 16) rows of stocking stitch on the 9 (10, 11) stitches of the instep, knitting together the last stitch of each row with the first stitch from the holder each time. Finish the row and cast off the remaining 43 (48, 53) sts.
Sew up the seam.

STRAP

Using 2.5mm (UK 12; US 2) needles and spicy red yarn, cast on 5 (5, 6) sts. Work 6cm (6.5cm, 6.5cm)/2⅜in (2½in, 2½in), i.e. 22 (24, 24) rows, in k1 p1 rib and cast off.
Sew the strap to the side of the sandal, 1cm (⅜in) from the instep.
Make a second sandal with the strap on the opposite side.

STRAWBERRIES (MAKE 2)

Using 3mm (UK 11; US 3) needles and scarlet yarn, cast on 7 sts. Work *k1, yon* 3 times and then k1.
Work 3 rows stocking stitch on these 13 stitches, working purl through back of loop over the yon on the first row.
Next row: K2tog across all stitches. Break off the yarn, thread the end through all remaining stitches, pull tight and fasten off.
Sew up the side, stuffing the berry with oddments of yarn. Embroider little seeds with cream-coloured yarn.

LEAVES (MAKE 2)

Using the 2.5mm (UK 12; US C/2) crochet hook and green yarn, crochet 10 chain (ch). Work 1 slip stitch (sl st) in the first stitch, 9 ch, 1 sl st in the previous sl st, 10 ch, 1 sl st in the last 2 sl sts, 9 ch, 1 sl st through the last 3 sl sts. Fasten off and sew one leaf to each strawberry.

FINISHING

Sew a strawberry with its leaf to the end of each strap and sew on the press stud underneath, using the photographs as a guide to positioning.

36 Flower Sandals

SIZES

3 months • 6 months (instructions for the larger size are given in brackets)

MATERIALS

1 ball each of Bergère de France Coton Fifty (or similar fine cotton-mix yarn) in Ficelle (string brown) and Bengale (spicy red) • 2.5mm (UK 12; US 2) and 3mm (UK 11; US 3) knitting needles • Stitch holder • 2.5mm (UK 12; US C/2) crochet hook • 2 small red buttons and 2 small green buttons

STITCHES

Double decrease, centred (sl2, k1, p2sso): See page 154.
Garter stitch: Knit every row.
Grafting: See page 155.
Single decrease, left slanted (sl1, k1, psso): See page 154.
Single decrease, right slanted (k2tog): See page 154.
Stocking stitch: Knit right-side rows, purl wrong-side rows.

GAUGE

26 sts and 37 rows in stocking stitch on 3mm (UK 11; US 3) knitting needles = 10 × 10cm (4 × 4in).

Note: Use smaller needles if your sample works out bigger than this; use bigger needles if your sample works out smaller.

METHOD

Start with the tongue.

Using brown yarn and 2.5mm (UK 12; US 2) needles, cast on 11 sts. Work 4 rows in garter stitch.

Row 5: K1, k2tog, k5, sl1, k1, psso, k1 [9 sts].
Row 6: Knit.
Row 7: K1, k2tog, k3, sl1, k1, psso, k1 [7 sts].
Row 8: Knit.
Row 9: K1, k2tog, k1, sl1, k1, psso, k1 [5 sts].
Row 10: Knit.
Row 11: K1, k3tog, k1 [3 sts].

Slip the remaining 3 stitches on to a stitch holder.

Pick up and knit 8 sts along the right edge of the tongue, knit the 3 sts from the holder and then pick up and knit 8 sts from the left edge of the tongue. Work 2 rows garter stitch on these 19 stitches and slip them on to a stitch holder.

Using 3mm (UK 11; US 3) needles and brown yarn, cast on 18 (20) sts, knit the 19 sts from the holder and then cast on 18 (20) sts [55 (59) sts]. Work 8 rows in stocking stitch. Change to 2.5mm (UK 12; US 2) needles and work 2 rows in garter stitch.

SOLE

Change to 3mm (UK 11; US 3) needles and work in stocking stitch, decreasing as follows: k5, sl2, k1, p2sso, k12 (14), sl2, k1, p2sso, k9, sl2, k1, p2sso, k12 (14), sl2, k1, p2sso, k5 [47 (51) sts].

Repeat these decreases so they lie one above the other on every second row 4 times and then graft the remaining stitches together (see page 155).

Sew up the back seam.

STRAP

Using 2.5mm (UK 12; US 2) needles and brown yarn, cast on 41 (45) sts. Work 2 rows in garter stitch.

Row 3: K2, k2tog, yon, knit to the end (this makes a buttonhole).

Work 2 more rows in garter stitch and cast off.

BACK LOOP

Using 2.5mm (UK 12; US 2) needles pick up 6 sts along the back of the bootie (3 sts either side of the seam). Work 14 rows garter stitch and cast off.

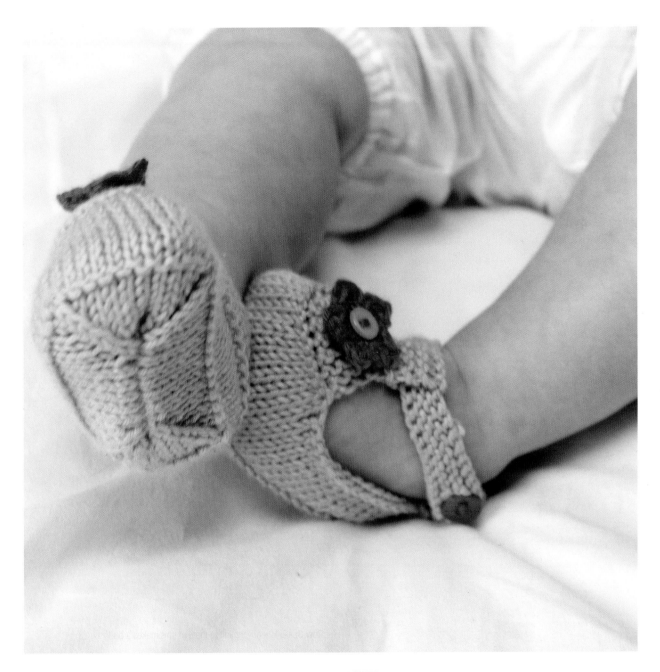

FRONT LOOP

Using 2.5mm (UK 12; US 2) needles, pick up 4 sts along the end of the tongue. Work 14 rows in garter stitch and cast off.

Turn over 1.5cm (⅝in) of the back and front loops and sew in place.
Thread the strap through the loops. Sew on the pink button to correspond with the buttonhole.

FLOWER

Using the 2.5mm (UK 12; US C/2) crochet hook, make a chain of 4 sts and close into a ring with a sl st.
Next round: Work *2ch, 1 htr (US hdc), 1tr (US dc), 2ch, 1 sl st,* in the ring, 5 times in all to make the 5 petals. Fasten off.
Sew the flower to the instep with the small green button in the centre.
Make a second sandal with the button and buttonhole on the opposite side.

37 Pink Princess Sandals

Pink Princess Sandals

SIZES

1 month • 3 months • 6 months (instructions for the two larger sizes are given in brackets)

MATERIALS

1 ball of Bergère de France Caline (or similar easy-care baby/fingering yarn) in Smoothie (pink) • 3mm (UK 11; US 3) knitting needles • 2 stitch holders • 50cm (½yd) of pink grosgrain ribbon with white spots, 10mm (⅜in) wide • 4 buttons

STITCHES

Single decrease, left slanted (sl1, k1, psso): See page 154.
Single decrease, right slanted (k2tog): See page 154.
Stocking stitch: Knit right-side rows, purl wrong-side rows.

GAUGE

27 sts and 36 rows in stocking stitch on 3mm (UK 11; US 3) knitting needles = 10 × 10cm (4 × 4in).
Note: Use smaller needles if your sample works out bigger than this; use bigger needles if your sample works out smaller.

METHOD

Start with the sole.

Using 3mm (UK 11; US 3) needles, cast on 10 (12, 12) sts. Work 6cm (6.5cm, 7cm)/2⅜in (2½in, 2¾in), i.e. 22 (24, 26) rows, of stocking stitch and slip the stitches on to a holder.

FOOT

Cast on 5 (6, 5) sts, pick up 17 (18, 20) sts along the left edge of the sole, knit the 10 (12, 12) sts from the holder, pick up 17 (18, 20) sts along the right edge of the sole and then cast on 5 (6, 6) sts [54 (60, 64) sts]. Work 2cm (2.5cm, 3cm)/¾in (1in, 1¼in), i.e. 8 (10, 12) rows, in stocking stitch on these stitches.

INSTEP AND SIDES

Row 1: K26 (29, 31), yon, k2tog, k3 (4, 4), k1, s1, psso. Slip the remaining 21 (23, 25) sts on to a holder and turn.
Row 2: P9 (11, 11), p2tog, slip the remaining stitches on to a holder and turn.
Row 3: K2 (3, 3), yon, k2tog, k2, yon, k2tog, k1 (2, 2), s1, knit the first stitch from the holder psso, turn.
Rows 4 and 6: P9 (11, 11), purl the next stitch together with the first stitch from the holder, turn.
Row 5: K4 (5, 5), yon k2tog, k3 (4, 4), s1 k1 psso, turn.
Row 7: K9 (11, 11), s1 k1 psso, turn.
For the largest size only, repeat row 4 and then work row 7 again.
Purl the 18 (20, 21) sts remaining on the left needle.
Cast off the remaining 47 (53, 55) sts, working purlwise on the right side of the work, and as you cast off, draw the edge in slightly by working as follows: p4 (3, 5), *p2tog, p5*, repeat from* to *.

Sew up the sandal.

STRAP

Using 3mm (UK 11; US 3) needles, 5 sts away from the instep, pick up 5 sts. Work 5.5cm (6cm, 6.5cm)/2¼in(2⅜in, 2½in), i.e. 20 (22, 24) rows, in stocking stitch, working a buttonhole (k1, k2tog, yon, k2) on the 17th (19th, 21st) row. Cast off.

FINISHING

Sew on the button.
Make a second sandal with the strap on the opposite side.
Cut the ribbon in half and tie a bow with each piece. Sew a bow with a button in the centre to each sandal, using the photographs as a guide to positioning. Trim the ends of the ribbon as desired.

38 Red Queen Sandals

SIZES
1 month • 3 months • 6 months (instructions for the two larger sizes are given in brackets)

MATERIALS
1 ball of Bergère de France Caline (or similar easy-care baby/fingering yarn) in Charlotte (red) • 2.5mm (UK 12; US 2) and 3mm (UK 11; US 3) knitting needles • Stitch holder • 50cm (½yd) of orange ribbon with red woven spots, 10mm (⅜in) wide • 2 buttons

STITCHES
Garter stitch: Knit every row.
Double decrease, left slanted (s1, k2tog, psso): See page 154.
Increase 1 (inc 1): See page 156.
Seed stitch (requires an odd number of sts):
  Row 1: *K1, p1*, repeat from * to * to the end, finishing with k1.
  Row 2: *p1, k1*, repeat from * to * to the end, finishing with p1.
  Repeat these two rows

GAUGE
27 sts and 36 rows in seed stitch on 3mm (UK 11; US 3) knitting needles = 10 × 10cm (4 × 4in).
Note: Use smaller needles if your sample works out bigger than this; use bigger needles if your sample works out smaller.

METHOD
Start with the sole.
Using 2.5mm (UK 12; US 2) needles and red yarn, cast on 35 (37, 39) sts.
Rows 1–2: Knit (work in garter stitch).
Row 3: K1, inc 1, k16 (17, 18) sts, inc 1, k1, inc 1, k16 (17, 18), inc 1, k1 [39 (41, 43) sts].
Row 4: Knit.
Row 5: K2, inc 1, k16 (17, 18) sts, inc 1, k3, inc 1, k16 (17, 18), inc 1, k2 [43 (45, 47) sts].
Row 6: Knit.
Repeat these increases 1 (2, 3) more time(s) every second row, knitting 1 more stitch at the beginning and end of the row and 2 more stitches between the 2nd and 3rd increases each time [47 (53, 59) sts].
Change to 3mm (UK 11; US 3) needles and work 10 rows in seed stitch on these stitches.

UPPER
Next row: In seed stitch, work 19 (21, 23) sts, s1 k2tog psso, work 3 (5, 7) sts, s1 k2tog psso, work 19 (21, 23) sts [43 (49, 55) sts].
Next row: Work in seed stitch.
Next row: In seed stitch, work 18 (20, 22) sts, s1 k2tog psso, work 1 (3, 5) st(s), s1 k2tog psso, work 18 (20, 22) sts [39 (45, 51) sts].
Next row: Work in seed stitch.
Continue decreasing in the same way, 1 (2, 2) more time(s), working 1 stitch less at the beginning and end of the row and 2 stitches less between the decreases [39 (41, 43) sts].

STRAP
K10 (11, 12) sts, cast off the next 19 sts, k10 (11, 12).
Change to 2.5mm (UK 12; US 2) needles and garter stitch. Slip the 10 (11, 12) sts on the right on to a stitch holder, work 4 rows on the 10 (11, 12) sts on the left and cast off.
Knit the 10 (11, 12) sts from the stitch holder and cast on 22 (23, 24) sts [32 (34, 36) sts].
Work 4 rows in garter stitch on these stitches, making a buttonhole (k1, k2tog, yon) on the second row, 3 stitches from the cast-on end. Cast off.

FINISHING
Sew up the sole and the back seam. Sew on the button.
Make a second sandal with the strap on the opposite side.
Cut the ribbon in half and tie each piece into a bow. Sew a bow to each sandal, using the photographs as a guide to positioning.

40 Two Little Mice

Cinderella Slippers

SIZES

Newborn/1 month • 3 months • 6 months (instructions for the two larger sizes are given in brackets)

MATERIALS

1 ball of Bergère de France Cotons Nature Plâtre (or similar fine, smooth natural crochet cotton) • 2.5mm (UK 12; US C/2) crochet hook

STITCHES

Abbreviations: Stitches (sts), chain (ch), slip stitch (sl st), single crochet (sc), double crochet (dc).

Crochet stitches: See pages 152–153.

Dc2tog: Insert hook in next st, yoh, pull through1 loop, insert hook in next st, pull through a second loop, yoh and pull through all 3 loops.

NB: dc is equivalent to sc in US terminology, i.e. UK dc = US sc.

METHOD

Start with the sole.

Using the 2.5mm (UK 12; US 2) crochet hook, chain 16 (18, 20) sts (includes the turning ch). You will be working around both sides of the chain.

Round 1: 1dc in the 2nd ch and each of the next 13 (15, 17) ch, 4 dc in last ch. Continue along the other side of the chain, working 1dc in each of the next 13 (15, 17) ch, 3dc in the last ch. Finish with a sl st in the ch at the start of the round.

Round 2: Sl st, 1dc in each of the next 14 (16, 18) sts, 2dc in each of the next 4 sts, 1dc in each of the next 13 (15, 17) sts, 2dc in each of the next 3 sts. Finish with a sl st in the ch at the start of the round.

Round 3: 1 ch, 1dc in each of the next 14 (16, 18) sts, *2dc in next st, 1dc in next st*, work from * to * 4 times, 1dc in each of the next 13 (15, 17) sts, work from * to * 3 times. Finish with a sl st in the ch at the start of the round.

Round 4: 1 ch, 1dc in each of the next 14 (16, 18) sts, *2dc in next st, 1dc in each of the next 2 sts*, work from * to * 4 times, 1dc in each of the next 13 (15, 17) sts, work from * to * 3 times. Finish with a sl st in the ch at the start of the round.

Rounds 5 and 6: 1 ch, 1dc in each stitch. Finish with a sl st in the ch at the start of the round.

Round 7: 1 ch, 1dc in each stitch, inserting the hook from back to front of work. Finish with a sl st in the ch at the start of the round and fasten off.

SIDES

Starting at the centre back, work 5 rounds in dc and finish off.

INSTEP

Work 1dc in the 12th (14th, 16th) stitch from the start of the side, 1dc in each of the next 10 sts, 3 × dc2tog, 1dc in each of the next 10 sts, turn, 1 ch, 1dc in next st, *dc2tog, 1dc in next st*, work from * to * 7 times, turn, 1 ch, * 1dc in next st, dc2tog*, work from * to * 5 times, turn, 1 ch, * 1dc in next st, dc2tog*, work from * to * 3 times, 1dc in last st and fasten off.

TIE

Make a chain 45cm (18in) long. Turn and sl st into each chain, but at around 22cm (8¾in) – about 1cm (⅜in) before the centre of the chain – work the next sl st into both the next st of the chain and the centre-back edge of the slipper. Work a sl st into each of the next 2 sts of both chain and slipper then continue by working a sl st into each remaining chain; fasten off.

Make a second slipper to match. Wrap the ties around the ankles when the slippers are being worn.

40 Two Little Mice

SIZES

3 months • 6 months (instructions for the larger size are given in brackets)

MATERIALS

1 ball of Bergère de France Cotons Nature Plâtre (or similar fine, smooth natural crochet cotton) • 2.5mm (UK 12; US 2) crochet hook • 1 length of brown embroidery thread • Tapestry needle

STITCHES

Abbreviations: Stitches (sts), chain (ch), slip stitch (sl st), single crochet (sc), double crochet (dc), half double crochet (hdc), half treble (htr), treble (tr), treble two stitches together (tr2tog).

Crochet stitches: See pages 152–153.

NB: The US equivalents of the terms used in the following instructions are as follow: dc = US sc, tr = US dc, htr = US hdc.

METHOD

Begin with the sole.

Using the 2.5mm (UK 12; US 2) crochet hook, chain 19 (22) sts.

Round 1: 1dc in the 2nd ch and each of the next 16 (19) ch, 3dc in last ch. Continue along the other side of chain, working 1dc in each of the next 17 (20) ch, 1 ch [38 (44) sts]. Finish with a sl st in the 1st dc of the round.

Round 2: 1 sl st, 2dc in 1st dc, 1dc in each of the next 16 (19) dcs, 2dc in next dc, 1dc in next dc, 2dc in next dc, 1dc in each of the next 16 (19) dc, 2dc in next dc, 1 ch, 1tr in the loop of 1 ch, 1 ch [44 (50) sts]. Finish with a sl st in the 1st dc of the round.

Round 3: 1 ch, 2dc in the 1st dc, 1dc in each of the next 18 (21) dc, 2dc in next dc, 1dc in next dc, 2dc in next dc, 1dc in each of the next 18 (21) dc, 2dc in next dc, 1 ch in the next tr, work 1 htr, 1tr and 1htr, 1 ch [50 (56) sts]. Finish with a sl st in the 1st dc of the round.

Round 4: 1 ch, 2dc in 1st dc, 1dc in each of the next 20 (23) dc, 2dc in next st, 1dc in next dc, 2dc in next dc, 1dc in each of the next 20 (23) sts, 2dc in next dc, 1 ch, 2htr in next htr, 1tr in next tr, 2htr in next htr, 1 ch [56 (62) sts]. Finish with a sl st in the 1st dc of the round.

Round 5: 1 ch, 2dc in 1st dc, 1dc in each of the next 22 (25) dc, 2dc in next st, 1dc in next dc, 2dc in next dc, 1dc in each of the next 22 (25) sts, 2dc in next dc, 1 ch, 1htr in each of next 2 htr, 3tr in next tr, 1htr in each of next 2 htr (hdc), 1 ch [62 (68) sts]. Finish with a sl st in the 1st dc of the round and fasten off.

SIDES

Round 1: 1 sl st at back of slipper (in the dc of the sole between the 2 × 2dc). 3 ch (replaces the 1st tr), then continue working around each st of the wrong side of the sole as follows: 1tr in each of the next 22 (25) sts, tr2tog (see page 153), 1tr in each of the next 5 sts, tr2tog, 1tr in each of the next 5 sts, tr2tog, 1tr in each of the next 23 (26) sts [59 (65) sts]. Finish with a sl st in the 3rd ch from the start of the round.

Round 2: 3 ch (replaces the 1st tr), 1tr in each of the next 21 (24) sts, tr2tog, 1tr in each of the next 4tr, tr3tog, 1tr in each of the next 4tr, tr2tog, 1tr in each of the next 22 (25) sts [55 (61) sts]. Finish with a sl st in the 3rd ch from the start of the round.

Round 3: 3 ch (replaces the 1st tr), 1tr in each of the next 20 (23) sts, 2 × tr2tog, 1tr in next tr, 2 × tr2tog, 1tr in next tr, 2 × tr2tog, 1tr in each of the next 20 (23) sts [49 (55) sts]. Finish with a sl st in the 3rd ch from the start of the round.

Round 4: 3 ch (replaces the 1st tr), 1tr in each of the next 18 (21) sts, 6 × tr2tog, 1tr in each of the next 18 (21) sts [43 (49) sts]. Finish with a sl st in the 3rd ch from the start of the round.

Round 5: 2ch, skip 1st 2tr, 1tr in next tr, *2ch, tr2tog, the first in the same st as the previous st and the 2nd in the 3rd following stitch*, work from * to * 5 (6) times, **1 ch, 2ch, tr2tog, the first in the same st as the previous st and the 2nd in the 3rd following stitch**, work from ** to ** 4 times, then work from * to * 5 (6) times. Finish with 1dc in the 2nd ch from the start of the round.

Round 6: 2ch, 1tr in the 1st group of 2tr, *2ch, tr2tog, the first in the same group of dc as the previous st and the 2nd in the 3rd following group of dc*, repeat from * to *, and finish with 2 ch, 1dc in the 2nd ch of the start of the round. Fasten off.

TAIL (MAKE 1 FOR EACH BOOTIE)

Make a chain of 6 sts and join with sl st into the 1st ch to form a ring. Now work in continuous rounds.

Round 1: 1 ch, 2dc in each of the 6 ch.

Round 2: 1dc in each of the 12 sts.

Round 3: 6 × tr2tog. Stop and cut the yarn 15cm (6in) from the last st.

Stuff the inside of the tail with leftover yarn. Thread the 15cm (6in) end through the 6 sts, pull tight and fasten off.

Sew the tail to the 4th round of the bootie.

EARS (MAKE 2 FOR EACH BOOTIE)

Make a chain of 10 sts, then work 1htr in the 3rd ch and each of the next 2 ch, 1tr in each of the next 2 ch, 3dc in last ch. Continue on the other side of the chain, working 1htr in the each of the next 2 ch, 1tr in each of the next 2 ch, 1htr in each of the next 4 ch and fasten off.

Sew an ear to the last round on each side of the bootie, 4cm (1½in) apart.

WHISKERS AND EYES

Cut four 7cm (2¾in) lengths of yarn, thread them together through the stitch at the centre front, at the bottom of the 3rd round, and tie in a knot.

Embroider the eyes in running stitch with the length of brown thread on the 4th round, 1.5cm (⅝in) apart.

Make a second slipper to match.

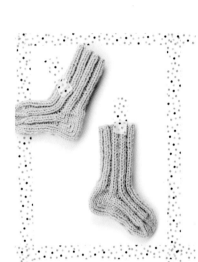

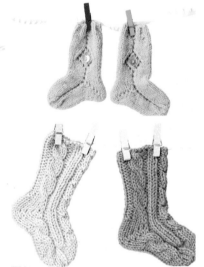

Cosy Socks

41 Lace Lovelies

42 Pink Diamonds

Lace Lovelies

SIZES

3 months • 6 months • 1 year • 2 years (instructions for the three larger sizes are given in brackets)

MATERIALS

1 ball of Bergère de France, Ciboulette (or similar easy-care baby/fingering yarn) in Diamant (white) • Set of four 2.5mm (UK 12; US 2) double-pointed needles • Stitch holder

STITCHES

Grafting: See page 155.

Lace rib (requires a number of sts divisible by 6 + 2):

Row 1 (right side): *K2, yon, k2tog, sl1, k1, psso, yon*, repeat from * to *, finishing with k2.

Row 2: Purl when working back and forth on 2 needles; knit when working in rounds on 4 needles.

Repeat these two rows/rounds.

Single decrease, left slanted (sl1, k1, psso): See page 154.

Single decrease, right slanted (k2tog): See page 154.

Stocking stitch: Knit right-side rows, purl wrong-side rows.

GAUGE

31 sts and 42 rows in stocking stitch on 2.5mm (UK 12; US 2) knitting needles = 10 × 10cm (4 × 4in).

Note: Use smaller needles if your sample works out bigger than this; use bigger needles if your sample works out smaller.

METHOD

Using a set of 2.5mm (UK 12; US 2) needles, cast on 30 (36, 42, 42) sts.

Work 5.5cm (6cm, 6.5cm, 7cm)/2¼in (2⅜in, 2½in, 2¾in), i.e. 24 (26, 28, 30) rounds, in lace rib.

Change to stocking stitch.

Next round: Knit, decreasing 0 (2, 4, 0) sts evenly over the round [30 (34, 38, 42) sts].

HEEL

Next round: Slip 8 (9, 10, 11) sts for the front and the first 8 (9, 10,11) sts of the round on to one needle. Leave the remaining 14 (16, 18, 20) sts on a stitch holder.

Work backwards and forwards in rows over the 16 (18, 20, 22) sts in stocking stitch, leaving 1 stitch unworked at the start of each row, until 4 (4, 6, 6) sts remain.

Now slowly pick up the stitches you left at the sides: working in stocking stitch, take in the first of the unworked stitches at the start of each row until you are back to 16 (18, 20, 22) sts.

FOOT

Slip the 14 (16, 18, 20) stitches from the holder back on to the needles [30 (34, 38, 42) sts]. Work 4cm (5cm, 6cm, 7cm)/1½in (2in, 2⅜in, 2¾in), i.e. 18 (22, 26, 30) rounds of stocking stitch on these stitches.

LACE RIB PATTERN

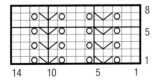

8

5

1

14 10 5 1

☐ 1 st stocking stitch

⊙ Yon (yarn over needle)

⊿ K2tog (knit two together)

◥ Sl1, k1, psso

TOE

Work in stocking stitch, starting the round at the middle of the stitches extending from the heel: k4 (5, 6, 7), sl1, k1, psso, k2, k2tog, k10 (12, 14, 16), sl1, k1, psso), k2, k2tog, k4 (5, 6, 7).

Repeat these decreases, positioning them above one another every second row twice and then every row until 12 (12, 16, 16) sts remain.

Graft the remaining stitches together (see page 155).

Make a second sock to match.

42 Pink Diamonds

SIZES

3 months • 6 months • 1 year (instructions for the two larger sizes are given in brackets)

MATERIALS

1 ball of Bergère de France Caline (or similar easy-care baby/fingering yarn) in Porcinet (piggy pink) • 2.5mm (UK 12; US 2) and 3mm (UK 11; US 3) knitting needles • 2 stitch holders • 2 small heart-shaped matching buttons

STITCHES

Grafting: See page 155.
K2 p2 rib: *K2, p2* repeat from * to *to the end.
Lace pattern: See chart.
Single decrease, left slanting (sl1, k1, psso): See page 154.
Single decrease, right slanted (k2tog): See page 154.
Stocking stitch: Knit right-side rows, purl wrong-side rows.

GAUGE

27 sts and 36 rows in stocking stitch on 3mm (UK 11; US 3) knitting needles = 10 × 10cm (4 × 4in).

Note: Use smaller needles if your sample works out bigger than this; use bigger needles if your sample works out smaller.

METHOD

Using 2.5mm (UK 12; US 2) needles, cast on 30 (34, 38) sts.
Work 6 (8, 10) rows, in k2 p2 rib.
Change to 3mm (UK 11; US 3) needles and work 6cm (6.5cm, 7cm)/2⅜in (2½in, 2¾in), i.e. 24 (26, 28) rows, in stocking stitch and lace pattern, following the chart, and positioning the yon after the 8th (10th, 12th) stitch.

HEEL

Next row: Slip the 22 (25, 28) sts on the left on to a stitch holder and work in stocking stitch on the 8 (9, 10) sts on the right, leaving aside 1 st at the middle end of the work on every second row 5 (5, 6) times [on the first row, leave 1 stitch unworked at the start of the round, the next time you start from the same direction leave 2 stitches unworked, then 3 and so on]. Continue until there are 3 (4, 4) sts remaining. This shapes the heel.
Now slowly pick up the stitches you left out: working in stocking stitch, take in the first of the unworked stitches at the start of every second row 5 (5, 6) times and then leave the 8 (9, 10) sts on a holder.
Knit the last 8 (9, 10) sts from the first holder and repeat the instructions for the first half of the heel.

FOOT

Using 3mm (UK 11; US 3) needles, knit all the stitches from the needle and stitch holders [30 (34, 38) sts]. Working in stocking stitch with the lace pattern, and keeping the line of holes continuous from the ankle and along the foot, work 4cm (5cm, 6cm)/1½in (2in, 2⅜in), i.e. 12 (16, 20) rows, on these stitches.

TOE

Continue in stocking stitch on 3mm (UK 11; US 3) needles as follows: k5 (6, 7), sl1, k1, psso, k2, k2tog, k8 (9, 10), sl1, k1, psso, k2, k2tog, k5 (6, 7). Rows start at the middle of the heel.
Repeat these decreases above one another every second row once and then every row until 10 (12, 14) sts remain.
Graft the remaining stitches together (see page 155).

FINISHING

Sew a narrow seam under the foot and up the back of the ankle. Sew a button in the middle of the diamond.
Make a second sock, placing the lace pattern on the opposite side of the ankle.

LACE DIAMOND PATTERN

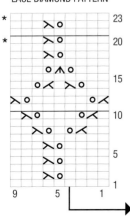

Size 3 months: 8th stitch
Size 6th months: 10th stitch
Size 1 year: 12th stitch

☐ 1 st stocking stitch

O Yon (yarn over needle)

╱ Sl1, k1, psso

╲ K2tog

⋀ Sl2, k1, p2sso

Repeat from * to *

43 Chain Cable Socks

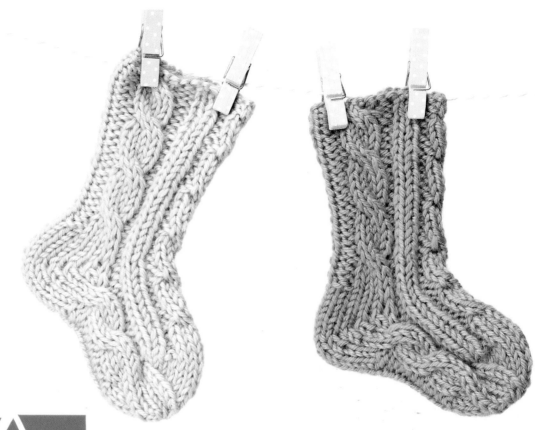

44 Cute Cable Socks

Chain Cable Socks

SIZES

3 months • 6 months • 1 year (instructions for the two larger sizes are given in brackets)

MATERIALS

1 ball of Bergère de France Idéal (or similar easy-care double knitting yarn) in Cyclamen (cyclamen red) or Meije (cream) • 3mm (UK 11; US 3) and 3.5mm (UK 9; US 4) knitting needles • 2 stitch holders • Cable needle

STITCHES

Cable left (see chart): Slip 2 sts on to the cable needle and leave at front of work. Knit the next 2 sts then knit the 2 sts from the cable needle.

Cable right (see chart): Slip 2 sts on to the cable needle and leave at back of work. Knit the next 2 sts then knit the 2 sts from the cable needle.

Grafting: See page 155.

K2 p2 rib: *K2, p2* repeat from * to * to the end.

P2tog: Purl two stitches together as one. This reduces the stitch count by one.

Reverse stocking stitch: Purl right-side rows, knit wrong-side rows.

Single decrease (sl1, k1, psso): See page 154.

Single decrease, right slanted (k2tog): See page 154.

Stocking stitch: Knit right-side rows, purl wrong-side rows.

GAUGE

24 sts and 31 rows in stocking stitch on 3.5mm (UK 9; US 4) knitting needles = 10 × 10cm (4 × 4in).

Note: Use smaller needles if your sample works out bigger than this; use bigger needles if your sample works out smaller.

METHOD

Using 3mm (UK 11; US 3) needles, cast on 32 (36, 40) sts.

Work 4 (6, 8) rows in k2 p2 rib.

Next row: Change to 3.5mm (UK 9; US 4) needles. Establish the pattern by working k2 (3, 4), p2, k8, p2, k4 (6, 8), p2, k8, p2, k2 (3, 4).

Work 5.5cm (6cm, 7cm)/2¼in (2⅜in, 2¾in), i.e. 22 (24, 28) rows, in cable pattern following the chart.

HEEL

Next row: Slip the 25 (28, 31) sts on the left on to a stitch holder and work in stocking stitch on the 7 (8, 9) sts on the right, leaving aside 1 st at the middle end of the work on every second row 4 (5, 6) times until there are 3 sts remaining [on the first row, leave 1 stitch unworked, the next time you start from the same direction leave 2 stitches unworked, then 3 and so on].

Now slowly pick up the stitches you left out: working in stocking stitch, take in the first of the unworked stitches at the start of every second row 4 (5, 6) times and then leave the 7 (8, 9) sts on a holder.

Knit the last 7 (8, 9) sts from the first holder and repeat the instructions for the first half of the heel.

FOOT

Knit all the stitches from the needles and holders [32 (36, 40) sts]. Continue in cable pattern following on from the ankle, and work 4cm (5cm, 6cm)/1½in (2in, 2⅜in), i.e. 12 (16, 20) rows, on these stitches.

TOE

Change to stocking stitch and work as follows: k5 (6, 7), sl1, k1, psso, k2, k2tog, k10 (12, 14), sl1, k1, psso, k2, k2tog, k5 (6, 7).

Repeat these decreases above one another every second row once and then every row until 12 (14, 16) sts remain.

Graft the remaining stitches together (see page 155).

FINISHING

Sew a narrow seam under the foot and up the back of the ankle.

Make a second sock to match.

CABLE CHART

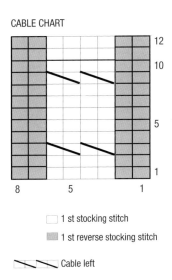

☐ 1 st stocking stitch

▨ 1 st reverse stocking stitch

⟋⟍⟋ Cable left

Cute Cable Socks

SIZES

3 months • 6 months • 1 year (instructions for the two larger sizes are given in brackets)

MATERIALS

1 ball of Bergère de France Idéal (or similar easy-care double knitting yarn) in Myosotis (sea blue) or Cendre (grey) • 3mm (UK 11; US 3) and 3.5mm (UK 9; US 4) knitting needles • 2 stitch holders • Cable needle

STITCHES

Cable left (see chart): Slip 2 sts on to the cable needle and leave at front of work. Knit the next 2 sts then knit the 2 sts from the cable needle.

Grafting: See page 155.

Reverse stocking stitch: Purl right-side rows, knit wrong-side rows.

Single decrease (sl1, k1, psso): See page 154.

Single decrease, right slanted (k2tog): See page 154.

Stocking stitch: Knit right-side rows, purl wrong-side rows.

GAUGE

24 sts and 31 rows in stocking stitch on 3.5mm (UK 9; US 4) knitting needles = 10 × 10cm (4 × 4in).

Note: Use smaller needles if your sample works out bigger than this; use bigger needles if your sample works out smaller.

METHOD

Using 3mm (UK 11; US 3) needles, cast on 32 (34, 36) sts.

Establish the pattern as follows: k2 (3, 4), p2, k4, p2, k2, p2, k4, p2, k2, p2, k4, p2, k2 (3, 4).

Work 2 rows of cable pattern on 3mm (UK 11; US 3) needles following the chart. Change to 3.5mm (UK 9; US 4) needles and continue in cable pattern until work measures 7cm (8cm, 9cm)/2¾in (3⅛in, 3½in), i.e. 24 (28, 32) rows in all.

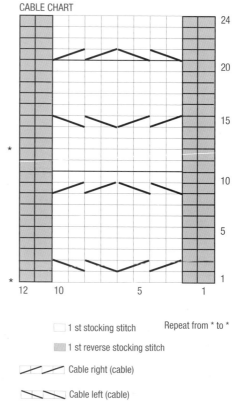

CABLE CHART

Repeat from * to *

□ 1 st stocking stitch

▨ 1 st reverse stocking stitch

⟋ Cable right (cable)

⟍ Cable left (cable)

HEEL

Next row: Slip the 25 (26, 27) sts on the left on to a holder and work on the 7 (8, 9) sts on the right, leaving aside 1 st at the middle end of the work on every second row 4 (5, 6) times [on the first row, leave 1 stitch unworked, the next time you start from the same direction leave 2 stitches unworked, then 3 and so on]. You will have 3 sts remaining.

Now slowly pick up the stitches you left out: working in stocking stitch, take in the first of the unworked stitches at the start of every second row 4 (5, 6) times and leave the 7 (8, 9) sts on a holder.

Knit the last 7 (8, 9) sts from the first holder and repeat the instructions for the first half of the heel.

FOOT

Knit all the stitches from the needle and holders [32 (34, 36) sts]. Continue in cable pattern, following on from the ankle, and work 12 (16, 20) rows on these stitches.

TOE

Change to stocking stitch and work as follows: k5 (6, 7), sl1, k1, psso, k2, k2tog, k10, sl1, k1, psso, k2, k2tog, k5 (6, 7).

Repeat these decreases above one another every second row once and then every row until 12 (14, 16) sts remain.

Graft the remaining stitches together (see page 155).

FINISHING

Sew a narrow seam under the foot and up the back of the ankle.

Make a second sock to match.

45 Simple Ribbed Socks

46 Striped Sensations

45 Simple Ribbed Socks

SIZES

Newborn/1 month • 3 months • 6 months (instructions for the two larger sizes are given in brackets)

MATERIALS

1 ball of Bergère de France Caline (or similar easy-care baby/fingering yarn) in Lutin (lime green) • 2.5mm (UK 12; US 2) and 3mm (UK 11; US 3) knitting needles • 2 stitch holders

STITCHES

Grafting: See page 155.
K2 p2 rib: *k2, p2*, repeat from * to * to the end.
Single decrease, left slanted (sl1, k1, psso): See page 154.
Single decrease, right slanted (k2tog): See page 154.
Stocking stitch: Knit right-side rows, purl wrong-side rows.

GAUGE

27 sts and 36 rows in stocking stitch on 3mm (UK 11; US 3) knitting needles = 10 × 10cm (4 × 4in).

Note: Use smaller needles if your sample works out bigger than this; use bigger needles if your sample works out smaller.

METHOD

Using 2.5mm (UK 12; US 2) needles, cast on 30 (34, 38) sts. Work 4 rows of k2 p2 rib.
Change to 3mm (UK 11; US 3) needles and continue in rib until work measures 5cm (6.5cm, 8cm), i.e. 18 (24, 30) rows.

HEEL

Next row: Slip 8 (9, 10) sts at each side on to stitch holders and work in stocking stitch on the 14 (16, 18) central stitches, leaving aside 1 st at the middle end of the work on every second row 4 (5, 6) times [on the first row, leave 1 stitch unworked, the next time you start from the same direction leave 2 stitches unworked, then 3 and so on]. You will have 6 sts remaining.
Now slowly pick up the stitches you left out: working in stocking stitch, take in the first of the unworked stitches at the start of every second row 4 (5, 6) times [14 (16, 18) sts].

FOOT

In the rib pattern, work the 8 (9, 10) sts from one holder, the central 14 (16, 18) sts and the 8 (9, 10) sts from the other holder [30 (34, 38) sts].
Work 3.5cm (4cm, 5cm)/1⅜in (1¼in, 2in), i.e. 12 (14, 18) rows, in k2 p2 rib, ending on a wrong-side row.

TOE

Change to stocking stitch and work as follows: k5 (6, 7), k2tog, (on subsequent wrong-side rows, work p2tog tlb), k2, s1, k1, psso, (on wrong-side rows, work p2tog tlb), k8 (10, 12), k2tog, k2, sl1, k1, psso, k5 (6, 7).
Repeat these decreases on each row, working 1 st less before the first decrease and after the last decrease and 2 sts less in the middle. When 14 (14, 18) sts remain, graft the remaining stitches together (see page 155).

FINISHING

Sew a narrow seam to join the sock.
Make a second sock to match.

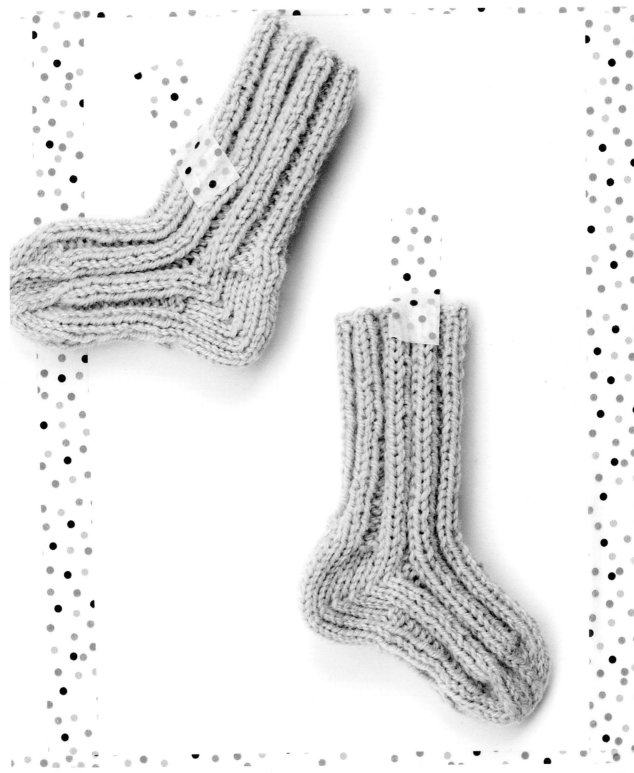

Striped Sensations

SIZES

Newborn • 1 month • 3 months • 6 months (instructions for the three larger sizes are given in brackets)

MATERIALS

1 ball each of Bergère de France Caline (or similar easy-care baby/fingering yarn) in Jerry (mid-grey), Bouba (chocolate brown), Charlotte (bright red), Baby (blue), Couffin (raspberry red), Lutin (lime green), and Kitty (fuchsia pink) • Set of 2.5mm (UK 12; US 2) and 3mm (UK 11; US 3) double-pointed needles, 20cm (8in) long • Stitch holder

STITCHES

Grafting: See page 155.

K1 p1 rib: *K1, p1*, repeat from * to * to the end.

Single decrease, left slanted (sl1, k1, psso): See page 154.

Single decrease, right slanted (k2tog): See page 154.

Stocking stitch: Knit right-side rows, purl wrong-side rows.

GAUGE

27 sts and 36 rows in stocking stitch on 3mm (UK 11; US 3) knitting needles = 10 × 10cm (4 × 4in).

Note: Use smaller needles if your sample works out bigger than this; use bigger needles if your sample works out smaller.

METHOD

Using 2.5mm (UK 12; US 2) needles and mid-grey yarn, cast on 26 (30, 34, 38) sts. Work 8 rounds of k1 p1 rib.

Change to the 3mm (UK 11; US 3) needles and work in rounds of stocking stitch. For the stripe sequence, work 2 rounds in each colour in the order brown, bright red, blue, raspberry, lime green, fuchsia and mid-grey. Start to repeat the sequence, as required, until you have worked 2cm (3cm, 4cm, 5cm)/¾in (1¼in, 1½in, 2in), i.e. 9 (12, 15, 18) rounds.

HEEL

Next row: Slip the last 6 (7, 8, 9) sts of the preceding round and the first 6 (7, 8, 9) sts of the new round on to one needle and leave the remaining 14 (16, 18, 20) sts on a holder.

Using blue yarn, work backwards and forwards in stocking stitch on the 12 (14, 16, 18) stitches, leaving 1 st at the beginning of each row unworked until 4 (6, 6, 8) sts remain in the middle.

Now slowly pick up the stitches you left out: working in stocking stitch, take in the first of the unworked stitches at the start of each row until you have 12 (14, 16, 18) sts again.

FOOT

Combine these stitches into a round with the 14 (16, 18, 20) sts from the holder [26 (30, 34, 38) sts] and work 3cm (4cm, 4.5cm, 5.5cm) 1¼in (1½in, 1¾in, 2¼in), i.e. 11 (14, 17, 20) rounds, in striped stocking stitch on these stitches. (Rounds should start at the centre of the heel and the stripes should continue in the established pattern).

TOE

Change to fuchsia pink and work as follows: k5 (6, 7, 8), k2tog, sl1, k1, psso, k9 (11, 13, 15), k2tog, sl1, k1, psso, k4 (5, 6, 7).

Repeat these decreases one above the other, working 1 st less at the beginning and end of the round and 2 sts less between the sets of decreases, on every second round twice, then on every round until 10 sts remain. Graft the remaining stitches together.

Make a second sock to match.

TIP

These socks do not require full balls of each colour so they are great for using up your leftovers from making some of the booties in this book. You can even play about with the colours you use on each sock – they don't have to be the same.

48 All Set

Red Razzmatazz

SIZES

3 months • 6 months • 1 year • 2 years (instructions for the three larger sizes are given in brackets)

MATERIALS

1 ball each of Bergère de France Caline (or similar easy-care baby/fingering yarn) in Carabosse (black), Kitty (fuchsia pink), Couffin (raspberry red), and Charlotte (bright red) • Set of 2.5mm (UK 12; US 2) and 3mm (UK 11; US 3) double-pointed needles, 20cm (8in) long • Stitch holder

STITCHES

Grafting: See page 155.
K2 p2 rib: *K1, p1*, repeat from * to * to the end.
Single decrease, left slanted (sl1, k1, psso): See page 154.
Single decrease, right slanted (k2tog): See page 154.
Stocking stitch: Knit right-side rows, purl wrong-side rows.

GAUGE

27 sts and 36 rows in stocking stitch on 3mm (UK 11; US 3) knitting needles = 10 × 10cm (4 × 4in).

Note: Use smaller needles if your sample works out bigger than this; use bigger needles if your sample works out smaller.

METHOD

Using 2.5mm (UK 12; US 2) needles and fuchsia yarn, cast on 28 (32, 36, 40) sts. Work in rounds of k2 p2 rib: 2 rounds in fuchsia, 2 rounds bright red and 2 rounds raspberry.

Change to the 3mm (UK 11; US 3) needles and work in rounds of stocking stitch: 2 rounds fuchsia, 2 rounds bright red and 2 rounds raspberry.

Change to black yarn and work 5cm (6cm, 7cm, 8cm)/2in (2⅜in, 2¾in, 3¼in), i.e. 22 (26, 30, 34) rounds, in stocking stitch.

HEEL

Next row: slip the last 7 (8, 9, 10) sts of the preceding round and the first 7 (8, 9, 10) sts of the new round on to one needle and leave the remaining 14 (16, 18, 20) sts on a stitch holder.

Change to bright red yarn and work backwards and forwards in stocking stitch on the 14 (16, 18, 20) stitches slipped on to one needle, leaving 1 st at the beginning of each row unworked until 4 (4, 6, 6) sts remain in the middle.

Now slowly pick up the stitches you left out: working in stocking stitch, take in the first of the unworked stitches at the start of each row until you have 14 (16, 18, 20) sts again.

FOOT

Using black yarn, combine these stitches into a round with the 14 (16, 18, 20) sts from the holder [28 (32, 36, 40) sts] and work 4cm (5cm, 6cm, 7cm)/1½in (2in, 2⅜in, 2¾in), i.e. 18 (22, 26, 30) rounds, in stocking stitch on these stitches. (Rounds should start at the centre of the heel).

TOE

Change to fuchsia and work as follows: k4 (5, 6, 7), sl1, k1, psso, k2, k2tog, k8 (10, 12, 14), sl1, k1, psso, k2, k2tog, k4 (5, 6, 7).

Repeat these decreases one above the other on every second round once, then on every round until 12 (12, 16, 16) sts remain. Graft the remaining stitches together (see page 155).

Make a second sock to match.

All Set

SIZES

3 months • 6 months • 1 year • 2 years (instructions for the three larger sizes are given in brackets)

MATERIALS

1 ball each of Bergère de France Barisienne (or similar easy-care double-knitting yarn) in Réglisse (dark brown), Jardin (leaf green), Papeete (turquoise blue) and Carotte (orange) • Set of 3mm (UK 11; US 3) and 3.5mm (UK 9; US 4) double-pointed knitting needles, 20cm (8in) long • Stitch holder

STITCHES

Grafting: See page 155.
K2 p2 rib: *K1, p1*, repeat from * to * to the end.
Single decrease, left slanted (sl1, k1, psso): See page 154.
Single decrease, right slanted (k2tog): See page 154.
Stocking stitch: Knit right-side rows, purl wrong-side rows.

GAUGE

22 sts and 30 rows in stocking stitch on 3.5mm (UK 9; US 4) knitting needles = 10 × 10cm (4 × 4in).
Note: Use smaller needles if your sample works out bigger than this; use bigger needles if your sample works out smaller.

METHOD

Using 3mm (UK 11; US 3) needles and green yarn, cast on 24 (28, 32, 36) sts. Work 6 rounds in k2 p2 rib.
Change to dark brown yarn and 3.5mm (UK 9; US 4) needles and work in rounds of stocking stitch.
Work 3.5cm (5cm, 6.5cm, 8cm)/1⅜in (2in, 2½in, 3¼in), i.e. 10 (15, 20, 24) rounds, in stocking stitch.

HEEL

Next row: Slip the last 6 (7, 8, 9) sts of the preceding round and the first 6 (7, 8, 9) sts of the new round on to one needle and leave the remaining 12 (14, 16, 18) sts on a stitch holder.
Using turquoise yarn, work backwards and forwards in stocking stitch on the 12 (14, 16, 18) stitches slipped on to one needle, leaving 1 st at the beginning of each row unworked until 4 (4, 4, 6) sts remain in the middle.
Now slowly pick up the stitches you left at the sides: working in stocking stitch, take in the first of the unworked stitches at the start of each row until you have 12 (14, 16, 18) sts again.

FOOT

Using dark brown yarn, combine these stitches into a round with the 12 (14, 16, 18) sts from the holder [24 (28, 32, 36) sts] and work 3cm (4cm, 5cm, 6cm)/1¼in (1½in, 2in, 2⅜in), i.e. 9 (12, 15, 18) rounds] in stocking stitch on these stitches. (Rounds should start at the centre of the heel).

TOE

Change to orange yarn and work as follows: k3 (4, 5, 6), sl1, k1, psso, k2, k2tog, k6 (8, 10, 12), sl1, k1, psso, k2, k2tog, k3 (4, 5, 6).
Repeat these decreases one above the other on every second round once, then on every round until 12 (12, 12, 16) sts remain. Graft the remaining stitches together.

Make a second sock to match.

49 Norwegians

50 Snow Stars

49 Norwegians

SIZES

3 months • 6 months • 1 year (instructions for the two larger sizes are given in brackets)

MATERIALS

Bergère de France Perfection in Lori (deep red) and Chèvre (cream), 1 ball each • 2.5mm (UK 12; US 2) and 3mm (UK 11; US 3) knitting needles • 2 stitch holders

STITCHES

Colour pattern: See chart.
Grafting: See page 155.
K2 p2 rib: *K2, p2*, repeat from * to * to the end.
Single decrease, left slanted (sl1, k1, psso): See page 154.
Single decrease, right slanted (k2tog): See page 154.
Stocking stitch: Knit right-side rows, purl wrong-side rows.

GAUGE

27 sts and 34 rows in stocking stitch on 3mm (UK 11; US 3) knitting needles = 10 × 10cm (4 × 4in).

Note: Use smaller needles if your sample works out bigger than this; use bigger needles if your sample works out smaller.

METHOD

Using 2.5mm (UK 12; US 2) needles and cream yarn, cast on 30 (34, 38) sts. Work 8 (10, 12 rows) in k2 p2 rib.

Change to 3mm (UK 11; US 3) needles and work in the colour pattern following the chart on page 149 for 9cm (9.5cm, 10cm)/3½in (3¾in, 4in), i.e. 28 (30, 32) rows. Work should measure 11cm (12cm, 13cm)/4¼in (4¾in, 5in) in total.

HEEL

Next row: Slip the 22 (25, 28) sts on the left on to a stitch holder and work in stocking stitch using red yarn on the 8 (9, 10) sts on the right, leaving aside 1 st at the middle end of the work on every second row 5 (5, 6) times [on the first row, leave 1 stitch unworked, the next time you start from the same direction leave 2 stitches unworked, then 3 and so on]. You will have 3 (4, 4) sts remaining.

Now slowly pick up the stitches you left out: working in stocking stitch, take in the first of the unworked stitches at the start of every second row 5 (5, 6) times [8 (9, 10) sts]. Slip these stitches on to a holder.

Return to the first 8 (9, 10) sts on the left and work the second half of the heel in the same way.

FOOT

Pick up the stitches from the holders [30 (34, 38) sts] and return to the colour pattern, continuing from where you left off. Work 4cm (5cm, 6cm)/1½in (2in, 2⅜in), i.e. 12 (16, 20) rows, in pattern on these stitches.

TOE

Using the red yarn only, work in stocking stitch as follows: (rows start at centre of heel) k5 (6, 7), sl1, k1, psso, k2, k2tog, k8 (10, 12), sl1, k1, psso, k2, k2tog, k5 (6, 7).

Repeat these decreases once on the second row, then on every row until 10 (12, 14) sts remain. Graft these stitches together.

FINISHING

Sew a narrow seam under the foot and up the ankle.
Make a second sock to match.

COLOUR PATTERN

Repeat from * to *

☐ 1 st cream

✕ 1 st red

Snow Stars

SIZES

3 months • 6 months • 1 year (instructions for the two larger sizes are given in brackets)

MATERIALS

1 ball each of Bergère de France Caline (or similar easy-care baby/fingering yarn) in Porcelaine (cream) and Spiderman (deep red) • 2.5mm (UK 12; US 2) and 3mm (UK 11; US 3) knitting needles • 2 stitch holders

STITCHES

Colour patterns: See charts.
Grafting: See page 155.
K1 p1 rib: *K1, p1*, repeat from * to * to the end.
Single decrease, left slanted (sl1, k1, psso): See page 154.
Single decrease, right slanted (k2tog): See page 154.
Stocking stitch: Knit right-side rows, purl wrong-side rows.

GAUGE

27 sts and 36 rows in stocking stitch on 3mm (UK 11; US 3) knitting needles = 10 × 10cm (4 × 4in).
Note: Use smaller needles if your sample works out bigger than this; use bigger needles if your sample works out smaller.

STAR PATTERN

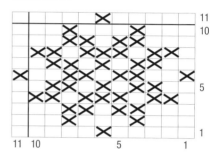

BORDER

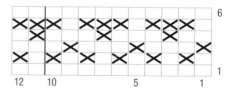

☐ 1 st red
✕ 1 st cream

METHOD

Using 2.5mm (UK 12; US 2) needles and cream yarn, cast on 30 (34, 38) sts. Work 5.5cm (6cm, 6.5cm)/2¼in (2⅜in, 2½in), i.e. 22 (24, 26) rows, in k1 p1 rib. Change to 3mm (UK 11; US 3) needles and red yarn and work 4 (6, 8) rows in stocking stitch.

Now work the star motif from the chart in cream, starting 3 (4, 5) sts from the right edge of the work.

Work a total of 5cm (6cm, 7cm)/2in (2⅜in, 2¾in), i.e. 20 (24, 28) rows, in stocking stitch.

HEEL

Next row: Slip the 22 (25, 28) sts on the left on to a stitch holder and work in stocking stitch in cream yarn on the 8 (9, 10) sts on the right, leaving aside 1 st at the middle end of the work on every second row 5 (5, 6) times [on the first row, leave 1 stitch unworked, the next time you start from the same direction leave 2 stitches unworked, then 3 and so on]. You will have 3 (4, 4) sts remaining.

Now slowly pick up the stitches you left out: working in stocking stitch, take in the first of the unworked stitches at the start of every second row 5 (5, 6) times [8 (9, 10) sts]. Slip these stitches on to a holder.

Return to the first 8 (9, 10) sts on the left and work the second half of the heel in the same way.

FOOT

Change to red yarn and pick up all the stitches from the holders [30 (34, 38) sts]. Work 3cm (4cm, 5cm) 1¼in (1½in, 2in), i.e. 10 (14, 18) rows, on these stitches, then work the border motif from the chart. Finish with 2 rows in red.

TOE

Change to cream yarn and work in stocking stitch as follows: (rows start at centre of heel) k5 (6, 7), sl1, k1, psso, k2, k2tog, k8 (10, 12), sl1, k1, psso, k2, k2tog, k5 (6, 7).

Repeat these decreases once on the second row, then on every row until 10 (12, 14) sts remain. Graft these stitches together.

FINISHING

Sew a narrow seam under the foot and up the ankle.

Make a second sock in the same way but with the star motif on the left side of the ankle.

Crochet Instructions

CHAIN (CH)

All crochet starts with a chain. Make a slip-knot loop. Insert the hook in the loop. Pass the yarn over the hook and pull it through the loop. Continue in the same way until you have the desired number of stitches.

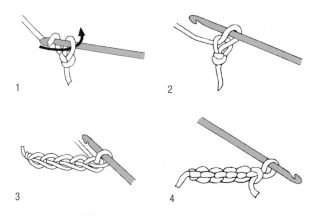

DOUBLE CROCHET (DC)/US SINGLE CROCHET (SC)

Insert the hook in a stitch. Pass the yarn over the hook and pull it through the stitch, pass the yarn round the hook again and pull through both loops on the hook.

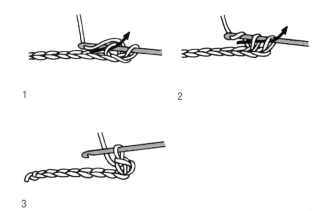

SLIP STITCH (SL ST)

Insert the hook in a stitch. Pass the yarn over the hook and pull it through the stitch and the loop on the hook at the same time.

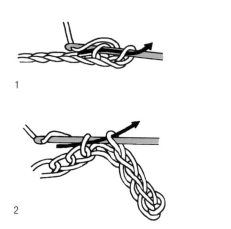

HALF TREBLE (HTR)/US HALF DOUBLE CROCHET (HDC)

Pass the yarn over the hook, insert the hook in a stitch and pull through, yarn over hook and pull through, yarn over hook and pull through all three loops.

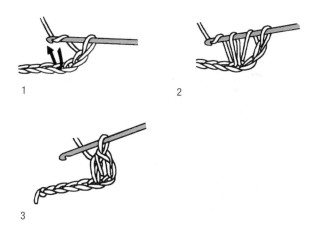

TREBLE (TR)/US DOUBLE CROCHET (DC)

Pass the yarn over the hook, insert the hook in a stitch, yarn over hook and pull through, yarn over hook and pull through the first 2 loops on hook, yarn over hook and pull through last 2 loops on hook.

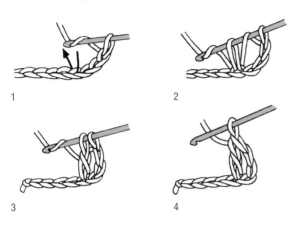

DOUBLE CROCHET TWO TOGETHER (DC2TOG)

Insert the hook in a stitch, yarn over hook, pull through 1 loop, insert the hook in the next stitch, yarn over hook, pull through 1 loop, yarn over hook, pull through all 3 loops.

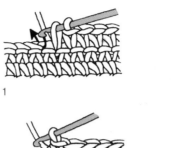

DOUBLE TREBLE (DTR)/US TRIPLE CROCHET

Pass the yarn over the hook twice, insert the hook in a stitch, yarn over hook, pull through 2 loops on hook, yarn over hook, pull through 2 loops on hook, yarn over hook, pull through last 2 loops on hook.

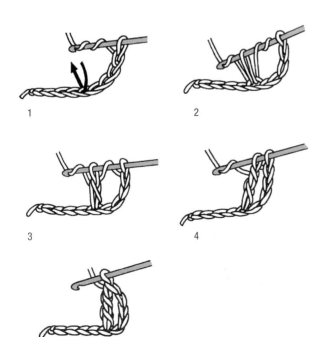

TREBLE CROCHET TWO TOGETHER (TR2TOG)

Pass the yarn over the hook, insert the hook in a stitch, yarn over hook, pull through 1 loop, yarn over hook, pull through 2 loops, yarn over hook, insert the hook in the next stitch, yarn over hook, pull through 1 loop, yarn over hook, pull through 2 loops, yarn over hook, pull through last 3 loops on hook.

Knitting Instructions

SINGLE DECREASE, RIGHT SLANTED (K2TOG)

Insert the right needle knitwise in the second stitch on the left and then in the first. Wrap the yarn round the right needle and pull it through both stitches in one movement. This decreases the stitch count by one. The decrease stitch slants to the right.

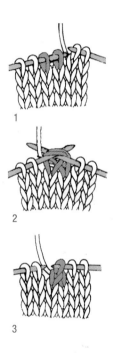

SWISS DARNING (DUPLICATE STITCH)

This clever stitch makes a good substitute for Fair Isle knitting when the motifs have only a few stitches and avoids the nuisance of carrying yarn across the back of the work. Use a tapestry needle and work from right to left. Insert the needle from the back of the work at the base of the first stitch over which you wish to work. Insert the needle from right to left under both threads of the stitch above the one you are covering (see fig 1), then reinsert it at the base of the stitch you are covering and bring it up again at the base of the next stitch to be covered (see fig. 2). Work all the stitches you need in the same way. After the last stitch in that row, bring the needle out at the base of the stitch in the row above. Turn the work round so that you always work from right to left.

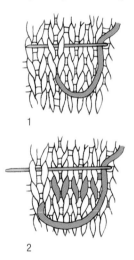

DOUBLE DECREASE, CENTRED (SL2, K1, P2SSO)

Slip 2 stitches from the left to the right needle, inserting the right needle as if you were going to knit two together. Knit the next stitch. Pass the two slipped stitches over the stitch just knitted. This decreases the stitch count by two.

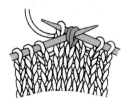

SINGLE DECREASE, LEFT SLANTED (SL1, K1, PSSO)

Slip a stitch on to the right needle by inserting it as if you were going to knit it. Knit the next stitch. Use the left needle to pull the slipped stitch over the stitch you have just knitted. This decreases the stitch count by one. The decrease stitch slants to the left.

DOUBLE DECREASE, LEFT SLANTED (SL1, K2TOG, PSSO)

Slip a stitch on to the right needle by inserting it as if you were going to knit it. Knit the next two stitches together. Use the left needle to pull the slipped stitch over the stitch you have just knitted. This decreases the stitch count by one.

1

2

3

GRAFTING

When you have finished knitting, do not cast off the stitches. Thread a tapestry needle with a length of yarn of the same colour as the knitting. Work with the right side facing you. Insert the needle in the centre of the 1st stitch and bring it out at the centre of the second stitch. Repeat this process with the first stitches on the other side. Continue in this way, releasing the stitches from the knitting needle/stitch holder as you sew them. This forms a row of stitches similar to a row of knitting, joining the two parts of the garment together.

1

2

INVISIBLE SEAM

Thread a tapestry needled with yarn of the same colour as the knitting. Work with the right side facing you. Lay the two pieces side by side, insert the needle along the horizontal line between the 1st and 2nd stitches on each side and pull tight enough to bring the edges together and hide the stitching. If the edges are very uneven, take the line between the 2nd and 3rd stitches. Shoulders can also be sewn together in this way. Take the two vertical strands of a stitch in a row at the edge of the work.

● ... Knitting Instructions

INCREASING EVENLY ACROSS A ROW – KNIT INTO THE ROW BELOW (K1B)

When you have to increase a row by several stitches, evenly spaced, divide the number of existing stitches by the number of extra stitches needed so you can space the increases evenly. Increase by knitting into the row below. Insert the right needle into the stitch below the next stitch on the left needle and knit it. Then knit the stitch from the left needle (figs 1–3). This process adds one extra stitch.

INCREASING AT A SPECIFIC POINT (MK1)

This kind of increase is done at a point one or more stitches from the end of a row. At the start of the row, knit 1 (or the number of stitches specified), pick up the bar between the stitches with the right needle and slip it on to the left needle (figs 4–5). Knit this through the back of the loop to twist it. This avoids a hole below the increase stitch. Continue the row. At the end of the row, when there is 1 stitch remaining on the left needle (or the number of stitches specified), pick up the bar between the stitches by inserting the left needle from the back and knitting normally, then knit the last stitch of the row (figs 6–7).

INCREASING AT THE VERY EDGE OF THE WORK

Add the desired number of stitches at the start of a row by making loops around the needle (fig 8). If you need to increase at the end of a row also, do the same at the end of the row. Knit these stitches in plain or purl or the stitch indicated in the pattern instructions (fig 9).

KNITTING ABBREVIATIONS

K: knit
P: purl
St: stitch
Inc: increase
Dec: decrease
K2tog: knit 2 together
Tbl: through back of loop
Sl1, k1, psso: slip 1, knit 1, pass the slipped stitch over
Sl2, k1, p2sso: slip 2, knit 1, pass both slipped stitches over
Yon: yarn over needle

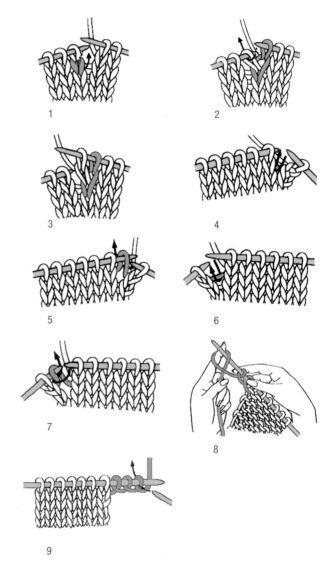

1

2

3

4

5

6

7

8

9

Acknowledgements

CASE, LACE DRESS, JEANS, GILET, TUNIC, FLOWERED LEGGINGS AND BABY TRAINERS: MONOPRIX

ERCUIS SILVER CUP AND AUBREY-CADORET NAPKIN RING: BERCEAU MAGIQUE

MINI WINDMILL AND UMBRELLA, CASE AND POMPONS: HEMA

RIBBON: MOKUBA

www.monoprix.fr – www.berceaumagique.com
www.hema.fr – www.mokuba.fr
www.truffaut.com – www.muskhane.fr
www.ferm-living.com – www.trousselier.fr

PLANTS, ARTIFICIAL GRASS AND CUT FLOWERS: TRUFFAUT

GEOMETRIC WALLPAPER AND HOUSE STICKERS: : FERM LIVING

FELT TORTOISES AND MUSHROOMS: MUSKHANE

SOFT TOYS: TROUSSELIER